SOULSPEAK

SOULSPEAK BY SUE SCHLESMAN
Published by Straight Street Books
an imprint of Lighthouse Publishing of the Carolinas
2333Barton Oaks Dr., Raleigh, NC 27614

ISBN: 978-1-64526-187-2

Available in print from your local bookstore, online, or from the publisher at: ShopLPC.com

For more information on this book and the author visit: www.susanwalleyschlesman.com

Brought to you by the creative team at Lighthouse Publishing of the Carolinas (LPCBooks.com):

Eddie Jones, Cindy Sproles, Shonda Savage, Amberlyn Dwinnell, Brian Cross, Elaina Lee

Libarary of Congress Cataloging-in-Publication Data
Schlesman, Sue.
Soulspeak, Sue Schlesman 1st ed

Printed in the United States of America

SOULSPEAK

PRAYING CHANGE INTO UNEXPECTED PLACES

Sue Schlesman

Straight Street Books
Lighthouse Publishing of the Carolinas

ENDORSEMENTS

When it comes to prayer, we need all the help we can get. *Soulspeak* will take your prayer life to the next level. Sue has written this book in a manner that is both practical and inspirational.

~ Mark Batterson
New York Times best-selling author of *The Circle Maker* and Lead Pastor of National Community Church

Soulspeak is literally the best book I've read in 10 years! I was hooked from the first paragraph. Sue hits the heart of what it actually means to follow Jesus. If you want to experience spiritual freedom and authenticity, *Soulspeak* will lead you into a deeper understanding of who God is and how to relate to Him.

~ Dr. Michael Smalley
Author, speaker, comedian, psychologist, founder of the Smalley Marriage Institute, Comedy of Love Marriage Event, and Smalley Marriage Radio

If you ever get the chance to meet Sue face to face, it will be a highlight to your day; reading her words is very close to that experience. A rare gift, her writing makes you feel that she is sitting right next to you, walking through difficult seasons with you like a friend who already knows every detail. I cried and laughed; I had to set the book down and walk away and think, then come back for more. I know for sure that *Soulspeak* will challenge you for your own good and for God's glory.

~ Jodi Oehlke-Cuccurese
Life Groups Pastor, James River Community Church

Sue Schlesman has made fire. From the first page to the last, *Soulspeak* will awaken your soul and bring you into the greatest personal revival of your life! The longer you walk with God, the easier it is to rely on your own brains instead of the Lord. If you're not careful, you can become very successful but natural-minded and weak. Then you find this amazing book and you remember how powerful God is, and how much he wants to be involved in your life.

~ Dr. Chuck Balsamo
Author, speaker, coach, Lead Pastor of Destiny Family Center

Honest. Sincere. Vulnerable. *Soulspeak* will encourage readers to rethink their approach to two important aspects of life—prayer and praise.

~ Larry J. Leech II
Author, writing coach

Soulspeak is the book on prayer we've all been waiting for. Sue Schlesman puts into words the longings of our hearts. She leads us to the ultimate authority and gives us a solid biblical foundation for building a strong prayer life. Definitely a book that will be a go-to present for those we love.

~ Edie Melson
Author, blogger, Director of the Blue Ridge
Mountains Christian Writers Conference

Soulspeak is one of the best books we've ever read on prayer. It takes prayer from the theological to the practical and doable. Sue's vulnerability, warmth, and biblical insights engaged us from Chapter One all the way through the book.

~ Brad and Heidi Mitchell
Co-Founders and speakers of Build Your Marriage

If you want to know God intimately, hear Him speak to you, and know how to speak to Him, grab a notebook and pen, and let *Soulspeak* speak to you. Sue Schlesman deftly weaves humor and wisdom as she shows the reader how their darkest moments can be redeemed by God's boundless love. *Soulspeak* reminds us all that God's greatest desire is to communicate His love to us, right down to our souls.

~ Renee Cobb
Speaker, author and founder of WOVEN
(Women Of Value in Every Nation)

Soulspeak: Praying Change into Unexpected Places by Sue Schlesman is a beautifully crafted book, which, as Sue states, "will pull you into God's embrace!" Let Sue help you find your patterns for prayer--your *soulspeak*. This book will bathe your soul as you draw near to God's heart through this honest format of connecting with Him.

~ Dee Dee Parker
author and editor

I started reading *Soulspeak*, and I couldn't put it down. Sue's writing style visually brings the stories of Scripture to life in your mind and heart. This book is an easy read with an impacting message about the power of prayer. I loved it!

~ Lisa Potter
Women in Leadership Director,
Potomac District, Assemblies of God

Sue's profound study moves people into a deeper understanding of prayer and its transforming effects on those who pray. She engagingly unlocks misunderstandings that prevent us from regular and effective prayer, moving us through the prayers progressively, with one building on another. Sue has a good grasp, both experientially as well as intellectually, on prayer. This is a great study for anyone who wishes to deepen her prayer life.

~ Marlyn DeFoggi
Author and Associate Pastor, West End Assembly of God

I began *Soulspeak* as a casual read, curious to see if Sue had anything different to offer on the subject of prayer. I began devouring multiple chapters at a time. As she shares her decades-long journey toward a deeper understanding and effectiveness in prayer, she clears a path for the rest of us. In each chapter she walks us through solid theology, shares transparent, real-life examples, and guides us into easy application. *Soulspeak* left me hopeful, inspired, and empowered. I can't wait to apply what I've learned.

~ Lori Hatcher
Editor of *Reach Out, Columbia* magazine,
award-winning author

Soulspeak focuses on the theology of presence. You will want to engage in prayer as you read the transparent personal narratives mixed with sound Biblical teachings and practical applications. Plan to keep this book close by as you develop your prayer life.

~ Dr. Bob Rhoden
Author, *Four Faces of a Leader*

FOREWARD

What a privilege it was, meeting Sue Schlesman, while teaching at The Billy Graham Training Center near Asheville, NC – years ago. I felt an instant soul connection as she shared about the call on her life to write a book on prayer.

To simply look at Sue, one would think, "I bet her life is perfect." But, nothing could be further from the truth. Sue's own personal Soulspeak success is evidenced by the way she wears the peace of God, like a beautiful garment, during some of life's most challenging and most painful life events. Thank you, Sue, for relentlessly pressing into the heart of God to provide this powerfully written, and much needed tool that will surely transform our thinking about prayer, and the way in which we pray, for the better.

It's a true honor to introduce you to my friend, Sue Schlesman. You will find her to be a woman of true beauty, courage, and prayerful grit. Thank you, Sue, for helping our souls learn to speak to God in deep and life changing ways.

LaTan Murphy
Writer, speaker, decorator, lover of people and strong coffee and author of *Courageous Women of the Bible*
www.lantanmurphy.com

DEDICATION

For Shane, Bruce, Brent, and Brady

You've blessed me with your love, let me love you,
and turned me into a prayer warrior.

I couldn't ask for more.

TABLE OF CONTENTS

ACKNOWLEDGEMENTS

I have spent years writing and rewriting this book, but that doesn't diminish the gratefulness I feel for the dozens of people who have encouraged and assisted me in turning my conviction into a book other people can read. I am humbled first of all by God's grace; I'm thankful for the thousand ways He speaks to me. I'm astounded that He doesn't grow weary when I don't hear His voice or respond like I should.

My biggest thanks goes to my family: my husband Shane for his unflagging support of my writing, Bible study, and speaking, not to mention his pleasant shrug when I've been writing all afternoon and forget to make dinner. I love you. You and Jesus are my rock. My three sons have also patiently supported my writing and ministry. Thank you—Bruce, Brent, and Brady. You are everything to me, even though you belong to God first. I'd also like to thank my mother, Barbara Walley, who instilled in me all that I am: student, teacher, Bible-lover, book-lover, writer, artist. I miss you, Mom. I hope you have books in heaven.

My agent, Diana Flegal and Hartline Literary Agency, took me on in faith and believed in this project even though prayer is a well-published topic. Thank you, Diana, for working hard to find *Soulspeak* a home. I'd be remiss not to mention my first writer friends, Cindy Sproles and Bob Hostetler, who affirmed my gift and encouraged me to leave my safe writing world to re-enter the rat race of publishing. LaTan Murphy, you are a soul sister; thank you for your many encouraging words. Thank you to Eddie Jones and Lighthouse Publishing of the Carolinas for publishing my first nonfiction book.

I'd like to thank my whole church, West End Assembly of God in Richmond, VA, for your support of me as a writer and teacher. Thank you to all the Bible study groups who have listened, discussed, and asked questions while I've taught the *Soulspeak* material. Your interactions with God's truth are priceless.

My friend list is too long to mention. You know who you are. We serve, eat, laugh, cry, pray, read and go on mission trips together. You have had a part in creating this book by affirming God's call on my life and by supporting me through your prayers. I also want to thank the people who gave me permission to tell their stories in *Soulspeak*. Besides my family, I'd like to thank Anna Smith, George Green, Misty King, Bill Stratton, Ed and Khristie Sinclair, and Crystal Hepburn. Each of my endorsers is a special friend to me; thank you so much for reading my manuscript and sticking your neck out for me. I pray God's blessings on your ministries.

And last—and perhaps most importantly—thank you, reader, for giving me a chance to speak into your life, for picking up this book and risking your soul to conviction and transformation. God will use something in here to blow down spiritual strongholds and release your praying power on the world. I admire you.

PART 1:
WHAT IS *SOULSPEAK?*

Many, Lord my God,
are the wonders you have done.
The things you planned for us,
No one can recount to you;
were I to speak and tell of them,
they would be too many to declare.
Psalm 40:5

CHAPTER 1
YEARNING

I GREW UP with the assumption that God would make my life happy if I were a good person. I'm sure no one specifically taught me that, but looking back, that was my conclusion. Good things happen to good people. Bad things happen to bad people.

Prayer seemed to be the grease that kept the Christian life machine running smoothly. I prayed at meals, bedtime, and crisis situations. I assumed that if I prayed and asked God to do good things, He would answer my prayers (because doing good is God's will, obviously). My theology proved true for a while because I grew up in a place where it was easy to be good and easy to be happy.

My Christian fantasy worked for a time. With a population of 10,000, my childhood hometown in southern Minnesota was large enough to entertain a good girl and small enough to keep me completely safe. It lay contentedly surrounded by a flat expanse of cornfields in every direction and was filled with shaded streets, sprawling Victorians with wrap-around porches, and big un-fenced front yards where kids like me actually played. Until dark. Unsupervised.

We enjoyed the freedom and safety of riding our bikes to the grocery for milk and to our friends' houses across town without ever wearing a helmet. Most families had only one car, and nobody wore a seatbelt. Even when normal winter temperatures plummeted below zero, kids bundled up and walked to school and played outside at recess.

And everybody was just fine. Life was really that idyllic.

Other than our parents' warnings about hippies, we didn't know anything about fear or stress.

I loved God a lot.

LEARNING TO YEARN

But as my adult life unfolded, I began a gnawing pursuit of reconciling God's will with my personal journey. I tried to wrap my innocent mind around why a good God allows pain to happen to good people. (A hard look at the real world will do that, won't it?)

I struggled with facing my pride, being real in my relationship with Jesus, praying even when I doubted, and believing my prayers could instigate change in a world where everything wasn't perfect. I began to share with God the inner whisperings of a heart that ached from disappointed dreams. Somewhere along life's road, things were not turning out for me like I had expected.

Have you experienced this dichotomy of faith? Do you wrestle with an innocent belief in a good God and a realistic understanding that bad stuff happens to good people all the time? That's when the doubt creeps in. That's when the desperation comes. And I suspect that's when God gets excited about what can happen to us next.

Prayer is the language of the desperate. Regardless of faith or creed, spiritual maturity or immaturity—prayer remains the intrinsic, universal language for the out-of-options, need-some-help-here population. Most of us pray when we don't know what else to do.

We post prayer requests on social media. We ask our pastors to pray for us. We utter desperate prayers in waiting rooms and church pews. We plead protection over our children. We pray over unpaid bills and grieving friends and anxious souls. We are oh so desperate.

Over the years, I have read David's prayers in the Psalms, and I always linger over his words in Psalm 84:2: "My soul yearns, even faints, for the courts of the Lord; my heart and my flesh cry out for the living God." This verse troubled me for some time because deep inside, I knew I was yearning, but I was pretty sure it had nothing to do with God's courts.

"What would it be like to yearn for heaven, instead of earth?"

What would it be like to yearn for heaven, instead of earth? What would it feel like for my soul to cry out for God—just God? The word for *yearn* in Hebrew is *kalah*, and it shakes my world. It's a verb meaning "to complete, consume, or accomplish, to be spent or exhausted, to put an end to." It's used in Scripture when God completes creation.

The same word shows up in a scene in Genesis: Abraham sends his servant back to Ur to find a wife for Isaac. After an arduous camel journey across what is now Syria and Iraq, the servant sits by a well and asks the first person he sees, a girl named Rebekah, for a drink. *Kalah* is used four times during this scene and twice in Genesis 24:19—"Now when she had given him a drink, she said, 'I'll draw water for your camels too, until *they have had enough to drink.*'"[1] Think of it! A camel can drink between 30-50 gallons of water at one time. A camel—or a desert traveler, for that matter—will *kalah* for water. They will keep drinking until they've had enough. *Yearn* means to drink deeply to completion—to thirst for water that satisfies and to not stop until the thirst is quenched, until the job is done. Until perfection.

Oh, how often I stop yearning after just one sip of God. I'm so anxious to return to my stressed-out life of false perfection that I convince myself I am satisfied with one sip of His

Spirit, one verse, one quick prayer for direction. But my soul craves more.

My blind pursuit for more is the reason I live with a lust for everything. It's why I have stress. Yet I conclude that my schedule is too full or the world is too evil. I don't recognize the yearning problem. My soul is speaking, but I am not listening.

Oh, yes. I am living in wild pursuit for something to satisfy. But what?

What does my soul yearn for? And what will satisfy it? I'm reminded of the story of Jesus and the Samaritan woman in John 4. Jesus seats Himself by the well to meet her, and when she comes to draw water, He asks for a drink. She is confused.

***

As a Samaritan and a woman, she can't fathom why a Jewish man, and a rabbi at that, would be speaking to her and asking for her help.

"Jesus answered her, 'If you knew the gift of God and who it is that asks you for a drink, you would have asked him and he would have given you living water.'

'Sir,' the woman said, 'you have nothing to draw with and the well is deep....'

Jesus answered, 'Everyone who drinks of this water will be thirsty again, but whoever drinks the water I give him will never thirst.'"

I am that woman. I am carrying heavy water jugs every day, trying to satisfy my insatiable thirst for more in a culture that never satisfies, while Jesus sits and offers me living water.

But I don't ask Him for living water. (I am already a believer, you know.) Instead, I make my prayers about me.

CHAPTER 2
DESPERATION

IF YOU'RE INTERESTED, I'd like to share with you my journey of becoming a woman of prayer—a woman who thirsts and drinks and is satisfied (except when I pick up my heavy jug and start the cycle again). I will show you how I took an honest look at my prayer life and determined to let my soul speak, instead of my mouth, how I stammer little prayers from my heart instead of my mind. I am learning to believe God hears me and that He will respond to me in His own way and His own timing. I am learning that His answer, whatever it is, will always be enough for me.

PREPARE YOURSELF
In Mark 5, we can read a short narrative about another woman, one who has suffered from continual bleeding for 12 years. All her resources have been spent seeking a cure, without success. Desperate for healing, she risks exposure and humiliation by joining the crowds that throng Jesus, calling His name, and asking for His help. She dares to be one of the multitude—even though her condition requires confinement—because she thirsts for relief.

The woman doesn't expect Jesus will hear her little voice in the din of so many urgent requests; neither does she presume that her needs are greater than anyone else's. She doesn't demand His full attention.

But she does hope His power can help her. She threads her way through the crowds, conscious of her bleeding and her need to reach Him quickly and return home. She quietly reaches out and touches the edge of His robe—she makes a brief connection with His undeniable power. She can't yet comprehend the value of standing exposed in God's presence. She just hopes that one quick touch will be enough to fulfill her deepest longings.

She wants a sip, but she gets so much more.

One touch, and her body instantaneously floods with healing. She feels the change. But Jesus wants her to feel more. He wants to give her living water that won't run out.

He turns and asks with authority, "Who touched me?" He doesn't allow her to slip back into the throng, to sneak home after one sip of His power. God craves our honest exposure. He knows that emotional healing occurs when a body entrusts itself into His power.

His disciples hear His question and chuckle, "Master, you are being mobbed! We can barely move in this crowd. What do you mean, 'Who touched me?'"

But Jesus has felt her heartache and heard her *soulspeak*. And more importantly, He wants her to recognize the yearning. "Someone touched me. I know that power has gone out from me."

The gig is up. Trembling, the woman comes forward.

I imagine Jesus smiles at her, in that loving, parental way we do when our children approach us in mortification, because He answers, "Daughter, your faith has healed you. Go in peace and be freed from your suffering." He doesn't just answer her request. He calls her "daughter." He connects Himself to her emotionally and relationally. Then He acknowledges her fears and alleviates her hopelessness. He heals the agony of her heart as well as her body.

It's always what Jesus does when we yearn for Him.

FINDING PRAYER, FINDING GOD

Desperation is a good teacher. I am learning to pray real prayers that invoke real change. I began praying, not because I knew I should, or because I wanted something, or even because I needed something. I began praying from my soul because I yearned to speak and be heard.

It's still the reason that I pray. I pray because I understand the limits of my own spirituality. I pray because I'm afraid my own shortcomings will ruin my children. I pray because I've experienced heartache and longing so acute that bitterness threatened to sink like a blade into the secret places of my heart and twist until it killed me.

I pray because I know the strongest of marriages are breakable in the enemy's hands; I've lived that fear, and it's where I learned to lean into the God-ache. No one but Jesus could have crawled into the hidden corners of my fragile agony and sat with me and held my hand during my most painful hours. Only Him.

I pray because the world assaults my family, weaving beautiful lies about self-image, success, and fulfillment. And because I'm old enough to know I can't control my future, I have resigned myself to pray about it. It's a crucial resignation and a holy calling.

It's the breathing of a soul that craves the eternal.

> "I pray because I understand the limits of my own spirituality."

THE QUEST TO PRAY BETTER

Tim Keller explains, "Prayer is both conversation and encounter with God. . . . We must know the awe of praising his glory, the intimacy of finding his grace, and the struggle of asking his help, all of which can lead us to know the spiritual reality of his presence."[2]

Prayer is hard work. I think that's why we keep reading books about it. We're hoping someone will offer a simple principle that motivates us to pray and equips us to cause dramatic change in everyone around us, a covering against the onslaughts of a spiritual enemy. We want to fireproof our lives, so we pray in careful consideration of the wording and the phrasing.

We fail to see that the act of praying itself is not a covering, but instead a ripping away of the cloak that conceals an anxious heart. *Soulspeak* pushes us into God's presence.

This is the decision the bleeding woman made. After years of seeing doctors and hiding in her house, she pursued Jesus. She pushed her way through the throngs of admirers and skeptics; she risked exposing her desperate longing and the vulnerability of her need. She craved His touch that much.

Frankly, I think we're afraid God can't handle a hard look at the emotional baggage of our inner longings. We're so afraid, we close our prayer books and stop sharing prayer requests; we create theology that says we're not worthy or that Jesus doesn't do miracles anymore.

It's simple and complex, this love connection with the God of heaven. If I'm in relationship with Jesus, and if I want to hear His voice and feel His power and see His hand on my life, I will be drawn into prayer. Prayer is the rope I will clutch, while God sits in the boat and pulls me calmly and safely toward Himself. Sometimes He drags me through the water, even though He could easily walk to me or grab me. He knows the dragging will strengthen my faith—it's how I will recognize the possibility of my drowning. Somewhere during that exchange of self-reliance for faith, the rescue changes my perspective.

I play a role in this complex union of the natural and supernatural. As I lift my *soulspeak* to Him, the intricacies of our connection unravel; I forget myself. As I reach for Him, my soul's cry leads me into community with the Trinity with Whom I was created to communicate.

I speak to God, and He speaks back.

DESPERATE TO SPEAK AND BE HEARD

No thank you, you say, because you don't like being desperate.

I don't, either. We like having a plan, a system, a how-to for becoming a better prayer warrior. In the following chapters, I'll offer a lot of practical suggestions and share some amazing true stories that showcase how Biblical prayers pull you into God's embrace. Maybe that will help the process.

Most importantly, we will grow our faith and our *soulspeak* by patterning our prayers after the transformative prayer patterns in the Bible. We will approach prayer in this order:

- Powerful prayers begin with praise
- Praise reveals my need for confession
- Confession and worship help me lament through life's painful moments
- Lamentation generates thankfulness
- Thanksgiving liberates my soul to make requests
- Making requests spurs my intercession for others
- My awareness of others' needs motivates me to engage in spiritual warfare

This progression through prayer prepares our heart to approach God with confidence and hope. You really can pray change into the unexpected places of your complex life.

Your prayers will work.

God hears heartfelt prayers, the ones muffled into a wet pillow or whispered in a hospital waiting room. He doesn't expect perfect hearts or perfect lives; in fact, He craves the opposite. He yearns for our perfection only through His Son Jesus.

All those early years of attempting to be Perfect, wasted! God desires worshippers, exposed and vulnerable. He loves the agonizing process of pulling imperfect people toward Himself.

The Bible is filled with countless stories of flawed individuals who, in a moment of desperation, turned to their only hope—God Almighty—and found that He carried no bitterness about helping them. God heard their *soulspeak*, their naked whispers launched into the frightful cosmos of wavering faith. And He responded.

So pray your raw prayers. Ask for a drink. Reach for His robe. Speak from a pained soul that longs for healing.

Then say, with the Psalmist, "These things I remember as I pour out my soul."

PART 2:
"YOU'RE AWESOME":
SPEAKING PRAISE

I will extol the Lord at all times; his praise
will always be on my lips.
My soul will boast in the Lord;
let the afflicted hear and rejoice.
Glorify the Lord with me; let us exalt his name together.
I sought the Lord, and he answered me;
he delivered me from all my fears.
Those who look to him are radiant;
their faces are never covered with shame.
This poor man called, and the Lord heard him;
he saved him out of all his troubles.
Psalm 34:1-6

CHAPTER 3
GRUELING WAIT

ONE STIFLING, LAZY Virginia day, I drove through an unfamiliar neighborhood after dropping a teenager off at her house. Crepe myrtles, heavy with fuchsia plumes, draped their boughs over the curb-lined street as I headed home. The road seemed to stretch forever in the summer afternoon haze.

I started to reach into the back seat for my purse and phone but reconsidered and placed both hands on the wheel. I considered turning on the radio for some tunes, but I decided instead to focus on watching for the turn. Something warned me that I should pay attention to the road.

Then it happened—a crash that sounded like two freight trains colliding. Metal crumpled, and glass shattered. A red blur flashed in my peripheral vision. I felt myself careening across the pavement, hands clutching a locked wheel, feet braced against the floor, while my body lurched forward and snapped back under the impact. The smell of burning sulfur filled the car.

Groggy, I looked through the cracked windshield. Twenty feet in front of me, a long twisted black bumper lay in the road, with my personalized license plate visible in the center.

Gray smoke leaked from the dashboard. My burned and bleeding arms still stretched toward the steering wheel, which now sported a deflated white pillow. Ahead of me, lodged in a white split-rail fence, was a red sedan, with wheels turned sideways and the hood crumpled.

People leapt from their cars and ran in its direction. My thoughts formed slowly. *I've been in an accident. I'm alive.*

Hands shaking, I reached behind my seat for my purse, fumbling for my phone. Without success, I tried a few times to call my husband Shane. My fingers trembled across the buttons, and the phone rattled in my hands.

A lady ran up to my window. "Are you alright?"

I nodded slowly. "Is the other person okay?" My words were slow and forced. My eyes drifted toward the red sedan.

"He's not breathing. There's a nurse here trying to revive him."

All I said was "Oh, God, no!" It was a desperate prayer that caught in my throat. The sky, seemingly dark with clouds, hovered like an unseen enemy threatening war. I was going to need a miracle.

I didn't get one. Not for a long time.

A living nightmare ensued. At the hospital, police questioned me, and two different nurses took blood—one for my hospital files and one for a criminal investigation.

In the hallway, the police officer whispered the tragic news to my husband: an elderly gentleman in a red sedan had crashed into my car's front right end and died at the scene.

We would soon realize that the accident was my fault. I had breezed through a two-way stop sign hidden by a blooming crepe myrtle. Multiple witnesses would tell the police and news reporters various stories: I was on the phone, I was traveling at 50 MPH, I was looking down at my lap. Although inaccurate, the news hit the local paper and evening broadcast with my name attached. I hid in my house, humiliated, afraid, and guilt-ridden.

A severe concussion caused me to talk slowly, move slowly, and forget nearly everything except that I might be going to jail. Post-traumatic stress disorder took over, and I began seeing a therapist. I met with police and lawyers. Through a fog, I watched my husband handle almost everything in my life—including housework, laundry, and the kids' activities. My family moved into crisis living, and anxiety overwhelmed me.

THE NEED FOR PRAISE

I craved to hear from God like never before. I prayed every moment I was awake and cognizant. You've probably had a crisis or two, so you know how good Christians work. We pray for our trials to resolve, and we look forward to praising God and sharing His miraculous story of deliverance after He rescues us. Then we breathe deeply and give God His deserved kudos.

What I had never understood until this tragedy was how much I failed to praise God *during* a crisis, while the outcome was still unknown. Previously in my life, all of my praising had occurred on the safe side of hardship. The thought of praising God in the midst of trouble seemed ludicrous. (Don't we need to wait and see how God answers our prayers first? Doesn't praise follow confirmation of an answered prayer?)

To this point, I had considered myself a real hero of the faith because I believed in God's power and omniscience. When I prayed, I said things like—"if it's Your will" or "according to Your perfect will"—just to let God know I understood how the prayer thing worked. But I had always withheld my praise until my issues were adequately resolved.

WHERE REAL PRAISE HAPPENS

The Bible mentions praising God about 400 times. In addition to the word *praise*, the Scripture's pages are studded with several hundred references to worship and God's glory. It would appear that God's highest purpose for creation is to bring glory to Himself. (Could that be why Jesus always talked about God's glory?) All creation is a living explanation of God's glory and goodness. But as long as God's children assess His goodness against the vacuum of our own needs, we will not bring Him glory, and our souls will not speak praise.

During my ordeal, I began to grasp that God desired my praise—not because of what it would do for Him—but because of what praising Him would do for me. (He's pretty secure in Himself without my approval). Praising God before I knew the outcome of my trial opened the door for me to enter heaven's throne room. It placed me at Jesus' feet, where all true worshippers belong.

Jesus explained this concept to the woman at the well when she gave excuses for her faithlessness. He said, "true worshipers will worship the Father in spirit and truth, for they are the kind of worshipers the Father seeks." We can't fake praise and worship. God sees through the rhetoric. When our praise reaches God, it does so from our most soulful place, from the inner sanctum of who we are and what we value. Only in a soul filled with wonder can adoration occur.

CHANGE OF FOCUS

Praise is foundational, because it demands that we focus on God rather than ourselves. Praise reveals who we are as worshipers and who God is as the Worshipped One. Your investigation of prayer can become a catalyst for regenerating your entire worship experience. Every hardship—great or small—is a magnifying glass; what you see through the lens of hardship will reveal what you believe; what you believe will be revealed by how you respond to that hardship—either through praise or through something else.

> "As long as we are assessing God's goodness against the vacuum of our own need, we will not bring Him glory, and our souls will not speak worship."

18

The oldest book in the Bible tells the story of Job, a spiritual man who lost all 10 of his children, his health, his wealth, and the encouragement of his friends. His incredible response to his calamity was, "Naked I came from my mother's womb and naked I will depart. The Lord gave and the Lord has taken away. May the name of the Lord be praised."

I know what you're thinking. *Well, isn't that nice? I'm not Job.*

Neither am I. But if we learn to pray praises to the Lord, we might begin to look like him.

Prayer is the avenue through which we can work out our confusion over what God is doing and what we should be doing. It's how we practice authentic conversation. Anyone can praise God at church. But praise is so much harder when you're desperate and alone. There, praise proves the intimacy of your relationship with God.

Job had to work this out, too. He debated his friends over his righteousness and argued with God, wrestling over the cause of his misfortune and God's responsibility to him as a godly man. The biggest challenge for Job lay not in surviving his trials, but in retaining his belief concerning God's character.

The real question—the one that burns deep in our souls—is not simply why should we pray, but why should we entrust God with our prayers? The pithy answer is that Job—and you—can make it through hard times if you have faith, but I'm not going to say that—because you will promptly close this book and call me an idiot.

I'm just going to suggest that strong faith arrives during the grueling wait. Job's response to calamity is radical because he actually survived his trial without receiving explanation for his misfortune. The writer of Hebrews pre-empted "faith living" by stating, "And without faith it is impossible to please God, because anyone who comes to him must believe that he exists and that he rewards those who earnestly seek him."[3]

God rewards the people who seek Him, not the people who get lucky with their prayers. He responds to the people who seek Him, who yearn for Him. And seeking involves trust.

You and I must trust God, which means trusting what He does and doesn't do. Daily circumstances present each of us with real dilemmas. We all have to answer the question: Will I praise God in any circumstance? Will I believe that His answer, which might not match mine, is always the right one?

If you're like me, you work hard to believe that what you're praying for will happen and what you're praying against won't happen. You pray with laser-like focus, while tapping your heels together. *I will believe. I will believe. I will believe.*

That's exhausting. And it's not real faith.

REAL FAITH

Hebrews 11:1 defines faith as, "Now faith is being sure of what we hope for and certain of what we do not see." It's not faith if you know how an ordeal will end. The process of planning, manipulating, and demanding perfect endings thwarts the supernatural. Every time you take control back from God, you trade an opportunity for the miraculous for certainty of the mundane.

Faith is intrinsically tied to what you believe about God and God alone. It has nothing to do with your positive outlook. We demonstrate our faith when our souls speak worship. Praise can only be faked for so long before you either believe what you're saying or you stop saying it. Paul explains trust like this: "So we fix our eyes not on what is seen, but on what is unseen, since what is seen is temporary, but what is unseen is eternal."

This is where praise steps up to the microphone. Praise will remind you that God's ways are higher than your ways, that His wisdom is infallible—that His care includes grace, love, and mercy. Praise and adoration of God benefits you, not God. He doesn't need your prayers of praise; He just knows the difference praise will make in your faith. When you focus on who God is, your wishes will stop interfering with your faith.

Try to praise God first—even when life looks bleak. Real faith will grow from your prayers and cultivate more praise in your life. No heel-clicking required.

PRAYER OF PRAISE

Are you a little worried about how to praise without asking for something or thanking God for blessing you? Try these two prayers—one from David, and then my personalized prayer taken from David's.

David's prayer: Psalm 8:1, 3-4
O Lord, our Lord, how majestic is your name in all the earth! . . . When I consider your heavens, the work of your fingers, the moon and the stars, which you have set in place, what is man that you are mindful of him, the son of man that you care for him?

My prayer from Psalm 8:
Dear Father, You are greatly to be praised! Your name is known in the whole world, and I praise You for the beautiful world that You created and the individuality of every human being! I am in awe of what You have done for me and what You are still doing in my life! In Your holy name, Amen.

CHAPTER 4
ADORATION

THE FACE OF ADORATION

When I first fell in love with my husband Shane, it wasn't hard to see his good qualities. Proof of his loving character popped up everywhere. Flowers, phone calls, gifts, cards, compliments. I received and appreciated all the attention; I hailed his praises in return. Everything he did pointed toward virtue. He was the most amazing guy in the world, and I adored him.

And then we got married. And went into the ministry. And had kids.

Remarkably, his life no longer revolved around pursuing and impressing me. He failed to tell me how beautiful I was every day. He didn't notice bulging diapers on the babies, overflowing trashcans, or messy floors. He usually provided thoughtful gestures at the appropriate holidays (birthday, Christmas, anniversary, Mother's Day), but the bulk of his activities surrounded working hard and establishing his career and ministry. I found less to praise and more to criticize because my adoration of him was so often tied to my desires, not to the sum of his character. I was so focused on what he should do for me, I had forgotten who he was. I had forgotten how to yearn for him because I was too busy yearning for attention.

It's the same with God. When we only praise Him for doing what we want Him to do, we ignore the real reason He deserves our praise: His character is love. It's flawless, sacrificial, and eternal. He has already conquered evil on our behalf. He has nothing else to prove to us.

PRAISE GIVES COURAGE

We must decide to adore, to trust what we know to be true, even when we cannot see it.

Mary praised God for her important appointment as Jesus' earthly mother in a familiar passage in Luke called "The Magnificat." She predicted that the people of the world would count her blessed, even though she was scared to death. (Remember, Gabriel's first instruction to her was "Don't be afraid.")

Although Mary was frightened and overwhelmed, she understood the principle of praising God for His character. Mary exalted the Lord for choosing her to be Christ's mother by quoting from the Old Testament at least 15 different times (this girl knew Scripture!). She recognized her position—"he has been mindful of the humble estate of his servant"—and God's position—"God my Savior" and "the Mighty One." For six verses, she recalled the generous deeds that the Lord had done in ages past, although nothing tangible had even happened yet on her behalf. She hadn't told her fiancé Joseph or her parents about the baby. The rumors about Jesus' conception had not started. (Her life was about to get really complicated!)

Adoration of God gave her the courage to perform her calling. It can give you courage, also. Speaking praise out loud in song or in prayer helps your mind believe what your heart knows to be true. When you pray with adoration, God's love gains a stronger foothold on your conscious thought. Praise will give you the courage to trust God, even when the outlook seems bleak.

MY COURT CASE

The fallout from my car accident was grim. I waited four months to go to trial in traffic court, where the extent of my guilt would either release me or land me in criminal court.

I tried desperately to pray, but I didn't even know what I should ask for. I couldn't change the events, and I couldn't manipulate the ramifications of the accident or the legal proceedings that needed to follow.

Hundreds of people prayed for me during those long months. Our church community wrote notes and brought meals over. They carpooled our kids. One dear friend took me grocery shopping every week. My lawyer received over 100 letters of character reference on my behalf.

Yet I still found it hard to attend church. Almost weekly, someone would stop me and say something like: "Look at you! You're perfectly fine!" They didn't know I could suffer a full-blown panic attack just emptying the dishwasher or that I couldn't remember the name of my youngest son's fifth-grade teacher.

I read and prayed my way through the many songs of despair penned by David when

"Speaking praise out loud in song or in prayer helps your mind believe what your heart knows to be true."

he was running from Saul and Absalom. It surprised me to read that David, in the midst of unfairness and oppression, repeatedly exalted his Lord and reiterated God's sovereignty and goodness. David had decided to trust, without knowing how his life would turn out.

With this example, I decided to trust the process God was taking me through. I trusted my history with God and His history with me. When I didn't have words, adoration became my *soulspeak* to God. Perhaps for the first time in my life, I forced myself to praise God for who He was instead of for what He did. I chose to believe that since God had always been good, He would be good again. My way out of the pit began and ended with God. My soul spoke Scripture to the Author's heart. After a few months of reading and speaking God's words back to Him, I began to believe them. For real. While I waited, I praised Him for who He was.

The answer to my requests for deliverance finally came. As I stood crying in the courtroom, God granted me mercy from the judge. The case ended in traffic court, and no criminal charges were filed. My ordeal had forced me to claim one great, simple truth: God is God, whether my life fulfills my expectations or not.

Did prayer change my situation? No doubt. But more importantly, it changed me. It sparked a new level of spiritual growth in my life. Praise made me willing to bring God glory, rather than worry about my own glory (or lack of it). The steps I took might help you make the same determination to worship the Lord, regardless of your life's circumstances.

SPEAKING PRAYERS OF PRAISE

To form *soulspeak* to God, it might be helpful to ask yourself these questions:

1. Who is He? (Relearn His character)
- He is loving, merciful, patient, omniscient, omnipresent, perfect, and just.
2. What does He do? (Review His actions)
- He creates, encourages, protects, heals, saves, consoles, empowers, strengthens, defends, judges righteously.
3. What has He done in the past for others and for you? (Remember His history)

- Read Biblical accounts.
- Write down your own history with God.

REVIEW OF PRAISE

- God is worthy of our praise because of who He is.
- You can't praise God if you don't trust Him.
- You can't pray effectively if you aren't willing to praise God before He does something.
- Use the Psalms to practice praising God.

PRAYER OF PRAISE

Getting the hang of praising? Pray through Moses' prayer of praise and my prayer of praise (or write your own!).

Moses' prayer: Psalm 90:1-2, 4
Lord, you have been our dwelling place throughout all generations. Before the mountains were born, or you brought forth the earth and the world from everlasting to everlasting you are God. ... For a thousand years in your sight are like a day that has just gone by, or like a watch in the night.

My prayer from Psalm 90:
Dear Father, You amaze and astound us with Your love and mercy. You have loved mankind for thousands of years, having mercy on us and redeeming us. You are willing to lengthen our days so that we can know You better. I am humbled by Your grace. Amen.

PART 3:
"MY BAD": SPEAKING CONFESSION

Then I acknowledged my sin to you and did not
cover up my iniquity.
I said, "I will confess my transgressions to the Lord"
—and you forgave the guilt of my sin.
Therefore, let everyone who is godly pray to you
while you may be found;
surely when the mighty waters rise,
they will not reach him.
You are my hiding place;
you will protect me from trouble.
Psalm 32:5-7

CHAPTER 5
THE BLAME GAME

I REMEMBER ONE rainy morning when I had two stupid arguments with two different people, both before 8:00 a.m. Not my finest moment.

The weather forecast on that eventful day was predicted sleet and freezing rain, followed by one to two inches of snow, beginning at 1:00 p.m. I live in Richmond, Virginia. Reports of snow usually generate school cancellations before any precipitation actually falls because central Virginians are terrified of snow and ice. We only have about six snowplows (all right, maybe a couple more), so a snow forecast makes big news. Everybody ransacks the grocery for milk and bread and stays inside for days.

This aspect of Southern culture is humorous to me because I grew up in Minnesota. When I was a kid, my mom kept a shovel inside the back door because we often shoveled our way out of the house in the morning. I'm not kidding. Even twenty degrees below zero and three feet of fresh snowfall couldn't keep us out of school unless the wind was blowing snow across the country roads.

Life in Virginia is quite different. Quite pampered, I might say. But I roll with it and buy extra water, bread, and milk at the appropriate times. Not really sure why.

During this particular Virginia winter, we'd already had two big snowstorms, six and eight inches respectively, which is more than we usually get in two years. Keep in mind—it had all melted rather quickly. Nevertheless, students had already logged about ten snow days, safely cloistered from the melting elements. In response to this latest forecast for sleet and snow, school officials announced a half-day schedule for the day in question, as forecasters expected the sleet to begin around noon. Students would go to school on time and be dismissed at lunch to avoid the impending weather.

I was relieved. My then-14-year-old son Brady could go to school in the morning, and I could get some things done before picking him up at lunch. So I went to bed late the night before because I was working on this manuscript, and I woke up early the next morning thinking about this manuscript. A peek through the blinds showed me only falling rain. Good. I wasn't getting up unnecessarily.

I dragged Brady out of his bed (literally) and began the awful morning routine of prepping a tired teenager who is not a morning person to leave the house for an activity he is not interested in on a day that he had hoped would become a snow day. I changed my clothes, brushed my hair, and warmed up the car. It was still raining. A few minutes past 7:00 a.m., we left the house.

As we crept down the wet streets, Brady reached for my phone (he didn't yet have an iPhone, so he was constantly confiscating mine) and said, "You have a message."

Sure enough, school had been cancelled at 6:15 that morning. That's fabulous news to a mom who's still in her jammies, but to a mom already on the road to school, this is dangerous information. I counted in my head how many hours of sleep I'd actually gotten the night before. Five! Feelings of deprivation and injustice welled up inside me.

"You had your phone on airplane mode, and the volume is off," Brady said.

"I didn't do that! I never turn off my volume! You're always the one turning it off. It drives me crazy. I'm so tired of you touching my phone!" I overreacted just a little.

"I didn't touch it. Dad must have turned it off."

Of course, he did! He was sleeping in today, and he didn't want my phone waking him up. I glared at the windshield, driving home through the now-freezing rain, fuming about Virginia weather. I entered the house and let the door slam just a little bit. I stomped around while Brady went back to bed, snuggled under warm covers, and immediately drifted off to sleep.

Of course, I couldn't go back to bed. I was angry. I went into my room for my slippers, letting the door close loudly on my way out. Then I began working on my manuscript (because I was in a perfect frame of mind to teach people about prayer).

I heard Shane get up, and I went in to ask innocently what he'd like for breakfast.

"Why did you slam the door?" he said with irritation.

"I didn't. You turned off my phone," I answered. "There's no school today, but I got up early and made Brady break-fast"—not really—"and got him ready for school and drove almost all the way"—not really—"then Brady looked at my phone and saw the volume was off and there was no school to-day! I can't believe you turned my volume off. I wish everyone would just leave my phone alone!"

"I didn't touch your phone. You're just mad you got up for no reason."

I am really too old to argue over something so stupid, but it happened. I apologized, eventually.

So what was my issue? Nothing big. I just knew I was correct when clearly, I was incorrect. My "rights" had been violated, and I wanted someone to blame. Isn't that the essence of any fight? Our highest priority is feeling validated in our own selfishness.

ENTITLEMENT

The modern generation that researchers call "Millennials" takes a routine beating from teachers and employers for being "entitled." That may be true, but before we jump on the bandwagon and proclaim Millennials the most self-absorbed generation ever, let's look at our history. Entitlement has been going on since Adam and Eve.

> "Entitlement negates our ability to praise and be thankful."

Mankind has been playing tug-of-war with God over whom to worship since Eve ate the proverbial apple. Eve's mindset of "I deserve this" deceived her into believing she could be independent of God; entitlement also gave Adam his alibi ("she gave it to me, so I ate it"). This attitude of "deserved blessing" has been interfering with relationships and worship ever since. Although we regularly fall out of a close relationship with God, we're pretty sure it isn't our fault.

This revealing narrative provides us some answers. Even though the evidence for human guilt is obvious, Adam and Eve both make excuses for their actions. They feel that someone else should be held responsible for their mistakes. They don't consider that their choices exclude them from fellowship with God. Like Adam and Eve, if we disrespect God's holy nature, we misunderstand that every sinful choice we make removes us from His presence and sends us down our own path, alone.

David spoke of the separation sin causes when he said, "If I had cherished sin in my heart, the Lord would not have listened." (Ps. 66:18) After repenting of his adultery with Bathsheba, he begged God, "Do not cast me from your presence or take your Holy Spirit from me." (Ps. 51:11). The word *cast* is translated "banish" in the New Living Translation. The Hebrew word is *shalak*, which means "to throw, cast, hurl, fling; to be thrown, cast out, or cast down." David viewed himself as worthless and vile in the sight of God, deserving of being thrown away like trash. Even after he'd confessed his sin, he still feared alienation from God. David dreaded that God would fling him away like the garbage he believed he was. Separated from God, David's heart would be deprived of *soulspeak* to his Heavenly Father. For David, craving forgiveness equaled craving God.

Here's a hard truth: honest confession obliterates excuses. We all know this, even if we've never thought of it before. It's why we don't like to confess what we've done. Until we admit our sin, we haven't repented of it. Until we repent of our sin, we remain in a broken relationship with God. As long as we are out of fellowship with God, we can't worship Him. Hence, we can't ask Him for anything (well, we can ask, but our prayers are powerless). Unanswered prayers are raining down all around us, and we blame God for not showing up in our time of need. We feel validated in our anger towards God.

The Blame Game has worked again.

ROADBLOCK TO CONFESSION

When it comes to confession, the real question is how much does entitlement interfere with our ability to confess? In society today, we are permitted to do almost anything if we have a plausible reason for it. We have even invented diseases and diagnoses to give medical credence for nearly all our dangerous or evil behavior.

Even in Christian culture, circumstances determine culpability; forgiveness hinges on our vague definitions of our rights, and happiness becomes the measuring stick. I deserve to have everything I want, and I deserve to be upset and mean when I'm deprived of what I deserve. Nothing should interfere with my happiness and attaining what I want should be easy. After all, God wants me to be happy.

Does He?

Really? Entitlement runs deep indeed.

Entitlement also negates our ability to praise and be thankful because entitlement focuses on self—what I need and what I want—which makes me unthankful and un-worshipful. Without God's perspective, we will all decide what we deserve, and we will all determine to get it to the detriment of everyone else.

DO THE TANGO

In elementary school, whenever a conflict broke out on the playground, teachers would step in with the interrogation "Who started this?" By-standing children would eagerly point out the initiators of the conflict. But that technique didn't work so well in my home. (After all, there were only two of us kids.) My mom always said, "It takes two to tango." I never knew how to tango, but I knew what she meant. *Own it. You are responsible for some part of this.*

James, who likely took the brunt for many a childhood conflict, since his big brother Jesus was perfect (how unfair!), lays out a simple explanation of how sin happens: "Each one is tempted when, by his own evil desire, he is dragged away and enticed." He follows up with the cure: "Confess your sins to each other and pray for each other that you may be healed."

But blaming someone else is a whole lot easier. Whenever my brother and I accused each other of doing something wrong, Mom would make her tango comment, and then she'd say, "Don't pass the buck!" I remember mouthing off once with "I don't have a buck!" But I knew what she meant by that, too. *Own it. You are responsible for some part of this.*

My mom would force us to say "sorry" to each other for whatever we had done. I recall rarely feeling sorry for anything. I only felt resentful because I had not yet taken responsibility for my part of the offense. Not until I had my own children did

I realize how crucial responsibility is to the confession, repentance, and restitution process.

Age doesn't change the problem. We will always feel indignant and justified for our actions if we focus on the wrong done to us; however, if we admit our own sins, remorse and embarrassment will follow. Then the guilt entwined in those emotions will push for restitution—doing or saying something that might make up for our sinful choices. No wonder this whole process of conscience, guilt, admission, confession, and forgiveness makes us uncomfortable! It's so much easier to pass the buck.

The "Who started it?"generation has birthed seven-year-olds who demand iPhones and young adults who expect $60,000/year for working at home in their pajamas. Everyone expects everything because they actually believe they deserve it.

If I'm being completely honest, I believe that I deserve whatever it is that I want. And when I want to be spiritual, I'm arrogant enough to believe that God should immediately give me what I want. This is not spirituality. It's the wrong side of spiritual warfare, and it will destroy my faith in a God who cares for me and who provides what I need, if I do not learn to own my disobedience and selfishness.

PRAYER OF CONFESSION

These aren't the easiest kind of prayers to pray. It might be easier to pray someone else's words until you get the hang of it. Try David's and my prayers of confession.

David's prayer: Psalm 51:1-4

Have mercy on me, O God, according to your unfailing love; according to your great compassion blot out my transgressions. Wash away all my iniquity and cleanse me from my sin. For I know my transgressions, and my sin is always before me.

Against you, you only, have I sinned and done what is evil in your sight, so that you are proved right when you speak and justified when you judge.

My prayer from Psalm 51:
Dear Lord, Please forgive me for my sin, according to Your unending love. Make my heart clean again—restore me to a right relationship with You. I don't want to be away from Your presence and Your blessing. Thank You for Your forgiveness. Amen.

CHAPTER 6
JUSTIFIED

"You started it!"

"No, you started it!"

The playground blame game continues to work, right into professional sports, the boardroom, the courtroom, the halls of Congress, and the White House. We are a country of childish adults, still pointing fingers and thinking we can fool the teacher. We think if we can deflect responsibility for our actions to someone who is even more responsible than we are, that means we are no longer guilty. We use the Blame Game to justify ourselves as if other people's sins make our own disappear.

The story of the Pharisee and the tax collector has changed my life, as well as my perspective on prayer. Because Jesus knew some in his audience "were confident of their own righteousness," He tells them a story about entitlement in Luke 18:9-14:

> "Two men went up to the temple to pray, one a Pharisee and the other a tax collector. The Pharisee stood up and prayed about himself: 'God, I thank you that I am not like other men—robbers, evildoers, adulterers—or even like this tax collector. I fast twice a week and give a tenth of all I get.'
>
> But the tax collector stood at a distance. He would not even look up to heaven, but beat his breast and said, "God, be merciful to me, a sinner."'

The Pharisee is a religious leader, for heaven's sake. Surely, he understands the need for repentance. He is responsible to the Jewish people for their spiritual understanding; yet his pride motivates his reason for prayer. Notice these marks of entitlement in his life:

- My prayer reminds God of how great I am
- I am a good person because I do good things
- I deserve to be blessed

The Pharisee's conclusion: *I have done all these good things for God, so He owes me whatever I want.*

The tax collector, however, is a Jew in the employment of the hated Roman government. He's not popular; yet his posture about himself contains neither defensiveness nor self-pity. Notice instead the marks of his confession:

- My prayer reminds me of how great God is
- I am a sinful person because I sin
- I deserve hell

The tax collector's conclusion: *God has done all these good things for me, so I owe Him whatever He wants.*

JUSTIFIED

Jesus explains the application clearly, so his self-righteous audience will get the point: "I tell you the truth, this man went home justified before God. For everyone who exalts himself will be humbled, and he who humbles himself will be exalted."

Justification is a mathematical term—a realignment of the ledger's columns to show a zero balance. Justification means a debt has been paid. The tax collector takes responsibility for his debt to God and asks forgiveness, garnering for himself a justified ledger of his sins. The Pharisee pretends the debt doesn't even exist.

How often do we pretend that nothing is spiritually amiss in our lives? That our difficulties at work and home do not stem from our own self-absorption?

James explains in his fourth chapter that the arguments and disagreements we regularly have in our lives come from our own selfishness and our own need to justify our actions, rather than correct them. We want what we don't have, so we manipulate until we can get it. We connive and abuse. But God's not fooled by our pointing fingers, and He's not answering any of our prayers.

The humble and righteous man, however, can pray for a miracle and get one. James explains the reason for that, too, in the very next verse: "Therefore, confess your sins one to another and pray for each other so that you may be healed. The prayer of a righteous man is powerful and effective."

"SAY THE SAME AS"

If I want to become a powerful prayer warrior whose prayers change the world (James promises that your prayers can make a sick person well), I need to be honest and humble about my position before God. "If we confess our sins, He is faithful and just and will forgive us our sins and purify us from all unrighteousness." Ah, the promise of perfection, if we only admit our imperfections!

The crux of the concept lies in the meaning of the word *confess*. In the Greek, *confess* means "to say the same as" or "to concede." I have to call my sin what God calls it, not what I want to call it. Turns out, my mom wasn't the only one who warned others not to "pass the buck." Wanting to remind himself that he could not blame anyone else for the decisions that came through his office, President Truman placed a plaque on his desk which read: "The buck stops here."[4]

Am I brave enough for the blame to stop on my desk? Or do I say things like:

"I'm sorry you took it that way."

"That's not what I meant."

"I'm sorry; I get my temper from my dad."

"You misunderstood me."

"I didn't mean to hurt anyone."

"If you hadn't _____, I wouldn't have _____."

"That's just my personality coming out."

"This happened because . . ."

Excuses. Buck-passing. Entitlement. *I'm not responsible. There's a good reason I behaved badly, and it's someone else's fault.*

We don't want to admit when we have been intentionally cruel, selfish, or rude because that would bring us shame and embarrassment. No one wants to say, "My bad." That would be admission of guilt.

Bingo! True confession initiates the quest for personal holiness, not diversion from the offense or a glossed-over apology. Real, honest-to-goodness confession commences radical change, a transformation from sinner to saint. Confession necessitates *soulspeak* into the omniscient mind of a God who is patiently awaiting opportunities to give unconditional grace. That's why God hears the prayers of the confessor. He longs to justify us so we can re-enter His holy presence. Any other substitution for holiness leaves us out of God's presence, out of His blessing, and praying the unproductive prayers of the frustrated.

COME ON IN

God awaits our confessions. He stands at the door of our hearts and knocks, waiting for us to let Him inside. Listen to how Jesus pleads with His wayward children: "Those whom I love I rebuke and discipline. So be earnest and repent. Here I am! I stand at the door and knock. If anyone hears my voice and opens the door, I will come in and eat with him, and he with me." When we live in sin, we close the door on Jesus and the relationship He offers us.

Although God is just and holy, His agenda is not judgment; He's not on a warpath to stamp out the sins of the earth. Jesus is on a quest to win our hearts—to catch up over a cup of coffee. This is God's *soulspeak* to us: Let me in! I want to share everything with you!

THE BIGGEST CONFESSION YOU COULD EVER MAKE

God knew the havoc that bitterness and blame would cause mankind, so He created a process for reconciliation. He modeled it through the entire Bible, beginning with the first sinners, Adam and Eve, when He confronted them for their sin and clarified their accusations. Because mankind broke the perfect relationship between Creator and creation, God planned a rescue—a reconciliation of eternal proportions.

He sent His son Jesus, at the perfect time in history, to enter the world as a human, live a sinless life, and be humiliated and killed as a criminal. Jesus then allowed God to restore Him to fellowship in heaven through a miraculous resurrection. This powerful conquest over life and death provided an avenue for imperfect mankind to be in relationship with a perfect Heavenly Father—through the intercessory sacrifice named Jesus.

The *soulspeak* for salvation (eternity with God) simply involves expressing your need for Jesus and your request of Him to take control of your life:

- Admit that you are a sinner (Rom. 3:23, 6:23)
- Believe that Jesus is God's Son and that He died for you (Jn. 3:16, Rom. 5:8-10)
- Confess that you want Him to become your Lord and Savior (Rom. 10:9-10, 13)

PRAYER FOR SALVATION

Your salvation prayer of confession might look something like this:

Dear Heavenly Father,

Thank You for sending Jesus to die on the cross for my sins. I'm sorry for trying to live my life for myself. Please forgive me for my sins. I want You to guide and direct my life from this moment on. In Jesus' name, Amen.

If you have prayed this type of *soulspeak*, you know peace and eternal security. You have also entered into a relationship with the God of heaven. That relationship, like any other, can be injured. God always forgives us, but He demands confession and repentance as prerequisites to a reconciled relationship.

CANCELLING OUT PRAYERS

You might not realize that avoiding confession immobilizes your prayers.

Jim Cymbala explains the scope of ignoring sinful habits in relation to prayer like this:[5]

> "Because Satan understands the potential of prayer far better than we, he has developed cunning strategies to clog the asking-receiving channel. An unforgiving spirit, bitterness, secret sexual sins—the list is endless—can stymie our praying. Every sin we hide and justify becomes a hindrance to bold, confident prayer to the Father."[5]

Ignored sin affects your mind and body, as well as your prayer life. Psalm 32 explains the physical detriments of overlooked sin, as well as the benefits of confession and forgiveness, with these phrases:

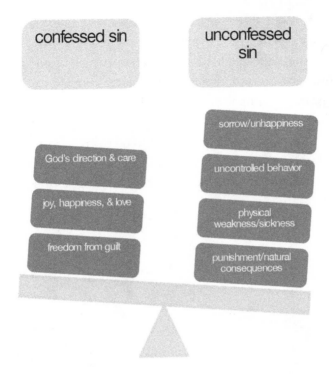

If we truly reverence and worship the God of the heavens, our natural response to Him will involve praise first and confession second. A lack of confession and repentance always reveals an absence of true worship. We can't expect to ever pray powerfully if we aren't willing to admit, confess, and reject the sinful patterns encroaching our lifestyles. Praying without confessing is akin to bailing out a boat on the ocean with a hole in the hull; make no mistake—the boat will eventually sink!

4 STEPS TO RECONCILIATION

Just like God is willing to reconcile us to Himself, we should make reconciliation with one another whenever offenses occur. Paul commanded in Col. 3:13, "Bear with each other and forgive whatever grievances you may have against one another. Forgive as the Lord forgave you."

When our three boys were little, we instituted the 1 John 1:9 policy. When the boys did something wrong, they had to name what they did, ask for forgiveness (which often involved restitution), and stop doing the sin. They also had to give forgiveness, if someone asked them. Usually, this process took a while.

I suspect you and I don't want to take this approach in our spiritual lives for the same reason that my children resisted it: the process is long and hard. The four steps are as follows:

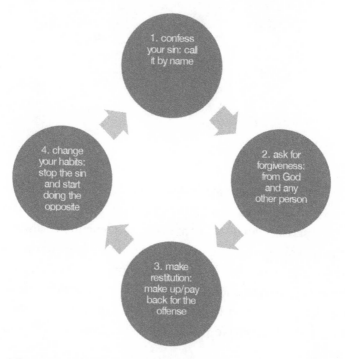

1. confess your sin: call it by name

2. ask for forgiveness: from God and any other person

3. make restitution: make up/pay back for the offense

4. change your habits: stop the sin and start doing the opposite

The reward of completing this process is life-changing! No grudges, no persisting hurt feelings, no misunderstanding, no bitterness. Confession and repentance will restore relationships. And relationship is why God created us in the first place.

HOW TO CONFESS

If this concept is overwhelming, here are some sentences to get you started toward accepting responsibility and gaining forgiveness whenever you sin:

- "It was my fault."
- "I'm sorry for _____." (the offense, not the reason)
- "Will you please forgive me?"
- "I will change. I will begin by doing _____."
- "How can I make this right?"

Look at the chart below to see how confession can replace the fruits of entitlement:

EXAMPLES OF ENTITLEMENT TURNED INTO CONFESSION

Statement of Entitlement	Prayer of Confession & Praise
I deserve to be happy	Lord, you are my joy and my salvation; in You only I have life. I confess my selfishness; make me an instrument of joy for others.
This isn't fair I don't deserve hardship	Lord, You are my rock and my redeemer; You will make beauty from ashes, so I will trust Your plan for my life. I want to focus on You, not myself.
I want this right now	Lord, I wait on You and your timing. You know what I need. I will trust Your will. Help me to be generous with what I already have and forgive me for my selfishness.

You break entitlement the same way you break a sin habit: confess, forsake, and replace it.

To practice confession, read two of David's prayers below and my prayer paraphrase. Use the elements of confession from Psalm 32 to form your own confessions.

REVIEW OF CONFESSION

- God won't hear your prayers if you don't confess your sins
- Confession means taking responsibility for what you've done
- Repentance means you want to change your sinful behavior and do the opposite
- Forgiveness gives freedom to both parties

PRAYER OF CONFESSION

Is it getting any easier? Try praying these two prayers of confession.

David's prayer: Psalm 41:4, 10-12
I said, "O Lord, have mercy on me; heal me, for I have sinned against you." . . . But you, O Lord, have mercy on me; raise me up, that I may repay them. I know that you are pleased with me, for my enemy does not triumph over me. In my integrity you uphold me and set me in your presence forever.

My prayer from Psalm 41:
Oh, Lord God, you are holy! I sinned against You when I _____. Please forgive me of this wrong and make me righteous again before You. Give me Your mercy! Please give me courage to ask forgiveness from _____ for my sin and give me the power of the Holy Spirit to root this out

of my life. I pray for the Holy Spirit to fight on my behalf and convict me when I have wrong thoughts or wrong motives. I will give You the honor and the praise for what You are doing in my life. In Jesus' name, Amen.

PART 4:
"LIFE STINKS": SPEAKING LAMENTATION

They have tracked me down; they now surround me,
With eyes alert, to throw me to the ground.
They are like a lion hungry for prey,
Like a great lion crouching in cover.
Rise up, O Lord, confront them, bring them down;
Rescue me from the wicked by your sword.
O Lord, by your hand save me from such men,
from men of this world whose reward is in this life.
You still the hunger of those you cherish;
their sons have plenty, and they store up
wealth for their children.
And I—in righteousness I will see your face;
when I awake, I will be satisfied with seeing your likeness.
Psalm 17:11-15

CHAPTER 7
WOE IS ME

MY HUSBAND AND I had been in youth ministry for seven years and pastoring for four years at a small, comfortable church in Virginia, when we decided Shane should finish his M.Div. degree. We were nicely settled in our first house with a newborn and a toddler. Against logic and our parents' counsel, we moved to Los Angeles, where a seminary had accepted all of Shane's transfer credits from his previous seminary. God's hand seemed to guide us through the entire process, as details about selling our stuff, renting out our home, and moving across the country were addressed and solved. It felt like a big adventure.

But wait.

Shane's job fell through after we arrived, and he went to work selling cars 60 hours/week and going to graduate school 20 hours/week, plus studying. He worked every weekend and every holiday, on straight commission, with no healthcare for six months. He left home at 7:30 and came home after midnight. We were running a deficit of $1,000 per month until his commissions began kicking in.

I stayed home alone with our two babies. Our newborn son was colicky, screaming around the clock and never sleeping more than 30 minutes at a stretch, even at night. I would walk around the house with him pressed against my chest, rocking and soothing him (when I really wanted to throw something instead). Postpartum depression and homesickness delivered a one-two punch to my emotions.

Any visit to the doctor presented a decision dilemma—colds, colic, immunizations—all required my best guess and cash up front. Since we didn't have any money, I often drove an hour into the desert to take the boys to the free Hispanic clinic (fortunately, the doctor spoke English). We also had only one car, which I normally didn't have, so small emergencies were out of the question.

We had no friends and no family near, except a college girlfriend who lived an hour and a half away (but once again, there was a car issue, so our visits were spread out). We began attending a huge church but struggled to make connections. Half the time, I went alone because Shane was working. I vividly remember my first Sunday in church there—I walked into the back of the sanctuary, stood in the aisle, and cried.

God was still present, even in my desperation. I joined a MOPS[6] group and made friends. Shane quickly climbed to the top of the dealership in sales and became the finance manager, and we began paying off our bills. We eventually bought a second car. So we were getting our prayers answered, right?

Actually, the spiritual warfare in our lives was palpable. Shane had taken control away from God in order to survive and provide. His work world was dark and oppressive. He felt betrayed by God, and he was angry about it. His childhood baggage resurfaced, along with dysfunctional coping mechanisms and feelings of abandonment.

Stress began dividing us. We were drowning, kicking our feet, and screaming for a lifeline, but nobody threw one out. Or at least we couldn't see to catch it.

Then Shane began going out with co-workers after work and staying out all night. Then he wanted out of our marriage. He became depressed, short-tempered, and sullen. He quit seminary. While he won awards at work, I watched my world spiral out of control. He began telling me I'd be better off if I divorced him. He had secretly decided he would leave us and quietly implode. He was lost.

I have never felt so desperate in my whole life. I prayed my guts out, while disgrace, shame, and anguish dominated my perspective. My faith tried to push past the lies. Through the power of intercession (more on that in Part 7) and loving confrontation by God, after a year of running, Shane stepped back from the brink of self-destruction and invited God back into his life. Although his repentance and healing would transpire gradually, he agreed to move back East with us and try to put back the pieces of our life.

Problem solved? No, now life got even messier.

As Shane healed and reality surfaced, I discovered betrayals, trauma, and my own part in my husband's unraveling. I questioned God about his love and justice. I raged. I sobbed. I brooded. I chastised myself. My prayers assumed a new kind of *soulspeak*—a gut-wrenching, no-idea-what-to-pray-for language of grief and hopelessness. I felt a total inability to pray, move forward, or express my feelings. I could only cry out to the Lord. Without realizing it, I had stumbled into a pattern of lamentation.

My laments stimulated an awakening inside my soul, a vulnerable romance between my heart and God's. Like never before, I felt His presence and His care for me, even amidst unsolvable problems. Sorrow ushered me into God's company, and my perspective began to change. Inside Jesus' intimate embrace, I caught a glimpse of the gospel—the real gospel— the kind that lies down and accepts anguish for the cause of Christ.

WHY LAMENT?

I've never heard a message or a lesson on how to lament in prayer.

Grief makes us uncomfortable. That might be why when someone sobs on our shoulder, we say things like "It'll be okay" and "You're gonna be fine." What we're really thinking is *Please stop crying. I don't know what to do.*

We can pray for people privately or hand them a tissue in prayer group, but laboring in verbal anguish is awkward for everyone. (Maybe I'm not the only one who thought the Christian life should make me happy?) Deep down, heartache challenges the validity of our faith. We'd rather confine grief to a funeral home than let it join our weekly Bible studies.

It's easy to forget that God's perspective embraces suffering. Jesus himself is called "a man of sorrows and acquainted with grief."[7] Jesus promises, "In this life you will have trouble. But take heart! I have overcome the world."[8]

To experience spiritual growth and powerful prayer, you must learn to lean into suffering. The enemy wants you to believe that maturity absconds with pain. He wants you sitting silently at home, separated from the family of God, spiraling downward into powerlessness. He wants you complaining about your pain, but not talking to God about it. Your spiritual enemy is no friend of lamentation. Here's why.

WEEP AND WAIL

The word *lament* means 'to cry out,' which is not the same thing as crying. *Crying out* suggests dependence and submission, as well as desperation, whereas *crying* can be associated with any number of causes. Crying (often mistaken for *whining* by teachers and parents) is closer to a complaint, whereas "crying out" is a lament. Ann Voskamp defines the spiritual difference between the two like this: *"Lament is a cry of belief in a good God, a God who has His ear to our hearts, a God who transfigures the ugly into beauty. Complaint is the bitter howl of unbelief in any benevolent God in this moment, a distrust in the love-beat of the Father's heart."*[9]

Although lamentation is a common Middle-Eastern expression, it is greatly misunderstood and under-utilized in the Western world. In Jerusalem today, orthodox Jews make pilgrimages to pray at the Kotel ha-Ma'aravi, the only original Temple wall still standing, which Gentiles call the "Wailing Wall." Lamenters place their written prayers between the limestone ashlars that form the wall's base. Their actions symbolize a transfer of control—a trust in God's perspective and power. They stand there to lament.

"The word lament means 'cry out,' which is not the same thing as crying."

The word *lament* means "to feel deep sorrow or express it by weeping or wailing; to mourn; to grieve."[10] Lamenting invokes the deepest, most raw emotions, the agonizing expression of loss and despondency that cannot imagine reprieve.

For thousands of years, previous generations have understood that grief required lamentation; in many cultures, professional mourners still attend funerals to cry and wail over the dead. I think the practice pays tribute to the grieving survivors as much as the deceased. Mourning validates emotions.

Without an outlet, grief will immobilize us. As a modern culture, we don't know how to grieve well, so doctors prescribe sedatives for grief, and therapists specialize in treating it. Instead of stepping into grief, we hide our feelings (e.g., medication), fight for justice (e.g., legislation), or take revenge (e.g., lawsuits). We've come to accept and believe that these techniques will grant us peace and closure over time. We are dangerously naïve.

A friend of mine recently retold me part of her husband's cancer story. She clearly remembers the day the doctor said her husband's melanoma had metastasized, and it was likely going to kill him. At the time, their twin boys were preschool age. She left the doctor's office and drove straight to our church to sit alone in the sanctuary. She wept. She wailed. She implored.

She questioned. She anguished. Her soul spoke the words she was too overwhelmed to utter. She just opened her heart's door to the Lord, and she unloaded her burden.

That's what God wants. He longs to sit with us in the darkness of an empty sanctuary and catch our words that fall like stars in the night sky. He longs to wrap His arms around us and hold us while we heave and sputter. He knows what to say and what not to say. He knows when to sit silently in the darkness, breathing in and out to our guttural groans. He doesn't sympathize with us—He actually *feels* us. It's why He bothered to come to earth in the first place.

PRAYER OF LAMENT

Ready? Feel free to lament to God. To make you more comfortable with it, pray David's prayer first, then try my version of it.

David's Prayer in Psalm 13:1-2, 5:
How long, O Lord? Will you forget me forever? How long will you hide your face from me? How long must I wrestle with my thoughts and every day have sorrow in my heart? How long will my enemy triumph over me? . . . But I trust in your unfailing love; my heart rejoices in your salvation. I will sing to the Lord, for he has been good to me.

My prayer from Psalm 13:
Dear Lord, I feel so disconnected from You. Please reveal Yourself to me. I'm so frustrated! I feel so alone. I don't want to believe that You have forgotten me. Draw me close and root out any sin in my heart so I can hear Your voice. I trust in Your love for me. I know that You will protect and guide me. You are so good to me, and I worship You.

CHAPTER 8
FREEDOM

I RECENTLY RETURNED from a mission trip to Costa Rica where my team and I spoke to girls and women about their worth in Christ. In the poor mountain villages there, girls in particular are at high risk for sexual assault by the men in their families: uncles, step-fathers, their mothers' live-in boyfriends, even their own fathers. Victimization becomes a part of the women's personal narratives and a factor in stifled dreams. The cycle of poverty and abuse continues from generation to generation.

My good friend Misty—whose formative years were also filled with abuse, trauma, and grief—accompanied me on this trip and courageously shared her personal story with the girls and women there.

When she spoke about being a victim of sexual abuse, I noticed girls hanging their heads in quiet shame. I watched women nod, their faces filled with pain. Shoulders shook silently. Women wiped their eyes and looked at Misty with hope, noting her smile and her tears. How could this young woman, so full of life and love, be happily married? Fulfilled? Content? Unafraid for herself and her children?

Misty spoke with bravery and compassion. She recounted how she, too, had cried out to God and asked, "Why me?"

She paused, with a smile and a tear. "Why *not* me?" Misty explained, "I began to understand that God had chosen me to bear great pain in my life because He was making me strong enough to handle it. My children will not endure what I endured. The cycle of abuse stops with me."

In the midst of unfair hardship and trauma, Misty has chosen to be a woman of courage. She has taken responsibility for her life, regardless of the blame she can rightly shift to other people, and she has made a choice to believe that God is big enough and good enough to manage her pain and transform her into a woman of faith and destiny. Her lament empowered her to change her focus and her destiny.

THE GREAT LAMENTERS

It's interesting that several of the human beings most intimate with God in the Old Testament were expert lamenters. Job, David, and Abraham pleaded and cried out to God on a regular basis; God responded to them with these incredible tributes:

Job: "There is no one on earth like him: he is blameless and upright, a man who fears God and shuns evil." (Job 1:8)

David: "The Lord has sought out a man after his own heart and appointed him leader." (1 Sam. 13:14)

Abraham: "'Abraham believed God, and it was credited to him as righteousness,' and he was called God's friend." (Jms. 2:23)

It would seem that lamentation and intimacy are entwined in an obscure relationship. Somehow, our anguish ties us to the heart of God. The Bible shows us how to wrestle with faith during the lamentation and grieving process. You might connect with Job's rant from Job 3, which I've paraphrased below. Maybe you've had a pity party like this one:

"I should never have been born! Or I should have died in childbirth! At least now I would be sleeping peacefully. Why bring me into the world and let me experience joy, only to snatch it away? That's cruel! I want to die, and yet You make me keep on living in misery! What kind of God are you? I have always been afraid something like this would happen, and now it has. I will never be happy again!"

The reason Job could wrestle with the question of God's goodness without forsaking his faith lies in the book's initial verse: "There once was a man named Job who lived in the land of Uz. He was blameless—a man of complete integrity. He feared God and stayed away from evil."[11] Lamenting doesn't dissolve Job's faith—it gives him a broader perspective about himself and his Creator. Before God exonerates Job in Chapter 42, Job has responded to God's rebuke with, "I know that you can do all things; no plan of yours can be thwarted... Surely I spoke of things I did not understand, things too wonderful for me to know... my ears had heard of you but now my eyes have seen you. Therefore, I despise myself and repent in dust and ashes."[12]

Through his loss, Job realizes to a greater degree that God doesn't owe him family, fortune, or happiness. Once Job shares God's perspective, he is free to lament, grow, and bask in the assurance that God loves him regardless of family or worldly goods. Job's righteousness gives him God's renewed blessing.

Job's lamentations produce clarity, praise, and repentance (even though he was practically perfect). Job's heart condition determines his type of response to adversity: lament or complaint. When our hearts believe God's words exclusively, the laments that pour out of us will be a sweet sacrifice, rather than an annoying noise. And that sacrifice of faith, which we make to God in the quiet misery of our souls, becomes an agent of change to countless people around us.

HEALING THE BROKENHEARTED

Have you ever said, "Why me?"

Of course. We all have.

But have you ever said, "Why *not* me?"

Perhaps God is gifting you with the highest calling possible—to suffer because of someone else. Jesus said, "Greater love has no one than this: that he lay down his life for his friends."[13] It took sacrificing God's only Son to break the chains of sin off this world. Perhaps it will take sacrificing your "perfect" life for you to break off the chains that bind someone in your family or the generations coming after you.

But when life seems unfair, don't believe the lie that God doesn't care about you, has forgotten you, or that you aren't good enough to deserve His protection. That is most certainly the kind of deception the enemy will speak over you when you struggle to break off spiritual chains. That's the lie he tells all of us. He wants us to believe that God has forsaken us, that we can't change, that our marriages are over, that our children are lost to us, that our pain is too great to bear, that we'll never be happy again.

The enemy's lies are strong, and they will romance your insecurities. You must decide to believe that God is love. The Bible's universal, over-arching theme is God's love for His creation. From Genesis to Revelation, all stories, genealogies, poetry, prophecy, history, and commandments point to God's love and his plan to reconcile mankind to himself through the sacrifice of His only son Jesus. He has no other plan for your life.

Because God loves you, He desires to hear your fears and complaints. He gives your soul both the longing and the need to speak. He is the perfect parent. If one of my children is overwhelmed with a struggle, my heart breaks not to hear him express it to me. I want him to pour out, to cry, and to rage about his life because I want to console him. I want to be close to him during the struggle.

> "That is how God woos us. He gives us grace. And he waits patiently for us to catch hold of it."

Like a mother who sits on the side of her weeping teen-ager's bed and listens, Jesus sits with us in our anguish, encouraging us to open up and dump everything on Him. David affirms, "The righteous cry out, and the Lord hears them; he delivers them from all their troubles. The Lord is close to the brokenhearted and saves those who are crushed in spirit."[14]

When Jesus began His public ministry, He quoted Isaiah in the temple. He spoke with supreme authority: "The Spirit of the Sovereign Lord is on me, because the Lord has anointed me to proclaim good news to the poor. He has sent me to bind up the brokenhearted, to proclaim freedom for the captives and release from darkness for the prisoners."[15] His intention in coming to earth has always been to free the captives and heal the brokenhearted. His will is to reverse the curse of sin on mankind.

HOW TO LAMENT

You might know how to lament to your friends and family. In your most comfortable surroundings, you can sometimes share your deepest burdens, your criticisms of others, and your complaints about the unfairness of life. But how might your soul respond if you felt free enough to lament before God, to spit out your anger and frustration at the only Person who can actually change things? Could you learn to lament like David, the Bible's best songwriter and expert worshipper?

David laments about his afflictions in more than 20 psalms![16] His laments typically begin with the problem in his life or a question he has about God's response to people's wickedness. But David's laments end with praise, a reassurance to himself of an eternal perspective, which defies human understanding. David verbalizes the reality of his situation, yet he lets God be God.

Jeremiah did too. So well, in fact, that he has carried the title "the weeping prophet" for thousands of years. Imprisoned in a deep pit, Jeremiah mourns the loss of his country and his people's faith throughout the book of Lamentations. Remarkably, Jeremiah comes to similar conclusions as David:

> "He has walled me in so I cannot escape; he has weighed me down with chains. Even when I call out or cry for help, he shuts out my prayer. . . Yet this I call to mind and therefore have hope: Because of the Lord's great love, we are not consumed, for his compassions never fail. They are new every morning; great is your faithfulness. I say to myself, 'The Lord is my portion, therefore I will wait for him.'"[17]

Each of the laments in the Bible includes some interesting characteristics that we could employ in our own prayers of lament. They include:

- questions about God's timing and responsiveness
- complaints about enemies or the world
- an awareness of waiting
- assurances of love and faithfulness to God
- requests for justice against my enemies, usually involving their destruction
- reminders of God's promises
- praise and adoration of God
- intercession for the downtrodden

A VISION

Several years after our return from California, an incident confronted me that required me to face the pain I'd buried. I was required to extend forgiveness again, or else grow bitter. I remember getting up in the middle of the night and lamenting to the Lord on my living room floor, crying my way through an entire box of tissues. Heartbroken, I searched the Scripture for some answers, some logical conclusions as to why I had to suffer. Buried deep within my *whys*, I discovered the core problem: I believed that I shouldn't suffer because of someone else's choices. I wanted to live my life by my own code of fairness: good people get good things and bad people get bad things.

All at once, the Lord gave me a clear picture in my head of Christ's crucifixion.

I saw a cross looming rugged against a night sky. The edges of the picture closed in, blurry like in a dream. Jesus was hanging there, His face contorted in pain, yet with eyes that were dark and compassionate. Thorns broke into His scalp, sending rivulets of blood down His sunken cheeks. His hands reached wide, pierced by heavy spikes, the skin tearing away from the hole in each. His face turned to mine, and I heard His voice, firm, yet tender:

"This wasn't fair.

But I did it for you.

I gave you grace when you didn't deserve it.

By this will all men know that you are my disciple, if you have love one for another.[18]

Greater love has no one than this that he lay down his life for his friends.

For God so loved the world that He gave His one and only Son …"[19]

Okay, okay. I get it.

Why *not* me? I threw away all the crumpled tissues and stood up. My pity party was over.

Another captive had been set free.

God will free you from the emotional scars and oppressive fears that hold you in bondage. God desires to draw each of us to Himself. His unbridled love propels Him toward a relationship with us, regardless of the personal cost to Himself. If we can accept His great gift, our life experiences will ultimately lead us into a deeper comprehension of God's overwhelming love. That is how God woos us. He gives grace. And He waits patiently for us to catch hold of it.

REVIEW OF LAMENTING

- Lamentation is not crying to God; it's crying out to God.
- Lamenting will encourage you to see God's perspective.
- God may be calling you to suffer because you are strong enough to break a cycle of sin.
- God desires to bind our wounds and heal our broken hearts.

PRAYERS OF LAMENT

You might like this one by Jeremiah when he's in a real predicament. Maybe you are, too.

Jeremiah's Prayer in Lamentations 3:46-47, 55, 57:
All our enemies have opened their mouths wide against us. We have suffered terror and pitfalls, ruin and destruction. Streams of tears flow from my eyes because my people are destroyed. . . . I called on your name, O Lord, from the depths of the pit. You heard my plea…. You came near when I called you, and you said, "Do not fear."

My prayer from Lamentations 3:
O Lord, I am so grieved! Everyone is against me! It's so terrible and so unfair! Come to my aid! Rescue me in Your perfect timing. I know You hear my prayers and You send Your spirit to comfort me. Give me the courage to not be afraid. I will trust in You! Amen.

PART 5: "THANKS A BUNCH": SPEAKING THANKS-GIVING

Shout to the Lord, all the earth.
Worship the Lord with gladness;
come before him with youthful songs.
Know that the Lord is God.
It is he who made us, and we are his;
We are people, the sheep of his pasture.
Enter his gates with thanksgiving
And his courts with praise;
Give thanks to him and praise his name.
For the Lord is good and his love endures forever;
His faithfulness continues
Through all generations.
Psalm 100

CHAPTER 9
WANTING MORE

My husband does not like the term "home improvement." His greatest fear is to come home to furniture rearranged or a room repainted—or worse yet, to a handyman tearing something out. He likes our home to remain predictably peaceful and unchanged.

I consider home improvement as self-expression. Art in progress. Inspiration unfolding. I have a good eye. I love to paint things, move things, buy things, repurpose things, and envision a better way to arrange and organize things. I have always been jealous of couples who agree on this matter—she dreams up a project, then he happily completes it. She points out closets without enough shelves, and *voila!*—an entire closet system with moving parts appears. She mentions that the kitchen functions poorly, and *voila!*—a renovated kitchen awaits her control. She wonders if two rooms would work better combined, and *voila!*—the wall comes down, opening up a wondrous floor plan. (Given my overuse of *voilas,* I might have some unconfessed bitterness in this area.)

You can see where this is going. As much as I am a creative, Shane is a pragmatist. To him, home improvement projects translate into discontentment, debt, and disturbance to an otherwise restful home front.

All of our homes have been old and in need of continual refurbishment. Plus there's me. So we have had a few issues in this department.

A few years back, I saved up for a big project I wanted done at our house and employed a handyman to take down the wall between our living room and kitchen and re-floor the dining area to match. I went to work figuring out how much wood flooring I needed, which wood to get, and how wide the planks should be.

Shane reluctantly agreed to the project. I assured him that after this, I would be content with the house.

The project began. Of course, it turned into a nightmare. The flooring levels of the rooms didn't match once we tore up the old carpet, so we had to tear up more flooring and add subflooring, all of which cost more money and more time. The electrical turned out to be a complicated fix, requiring additional electricians to get involved. We had issues in all the transition areas.

Meanwhile, we were living in a quarter of our downstairs, surrounded by stacked chairs, couches, and tables. We ate standing up around the kitchen sink. Nobody was happy.

Then the new flooring went down. I was so proud of myself for having picked an unvarnished floor (the least expensive option), at a flooring outlet, all by myself. I hired a guy with an electric power sander to come sand off the old floor's finish so we could varnish and poly everything to match. At this point, I called in a technician from a well-reputed flooring store in our area who came over to look at the job and help me pick the stain color.

"This is not the right floor," he said after one glance at my new dining area.

I almost threw up. "What do you mean?"

"Did anyone come out and look at your old floor or just show you samples? This is white oak. You bought rough red pine. Because of the grain, the color, and the knots, both sides are gonna look completely different."

I remembered, with nausea, that I had picked out the wood all by myself, looking at samples. (I have a good eye, remember.)

"Isn't there a way to make them match?"

"Not really. It's too bad they're in the same room. It wouldn't be as bad in a different room."

He left, and I bawled my head off for two days. I felt ashamed. I did.

While embarrassment and mistakes go hand-in-hand, shame is a different animal than embarrassment. Shame unmasks the motive behind a "mistake." I felt shame over my flooring mistake because I had been attempting to hide my pride and discontentment under an "artistic flair." The real me—the selfish, materialist me—had been de-robed, and I was ugly. This project wasn't about creativity; it was about wanting something *better*. All that time and money, which I could never replace, were wasted because I had determined not to be thankful for what I already had. I had convinced myself that I needed *more*.

Every time we purchase something, we practically recite in our heads: *It's not a sin to have more. It's not a sin to have more.* We convince ourselves that living with excess is preferable, as long as we tithe, give to missions, or say "thank you" before we eat or sleep.

What we fail to see is that we are like fish, opening our mouths for food—no one faults us for that—but we forget with our little fish brains that the food is actually bait. Hidden inside each mouthful sits a hook, carefully wedged, with a little barb on the tip to keep the hook in place. And we foolishly chow down. Having more is not a sin but *wanting more* is. *And it hooks us for life.* Only a rare fish can take the bait and swim away without getting hooked. *Wanting more* is the Devil's bait.

Discontentment in my life equals distrusting God's will for

my life. As long as I crave for more of anything other than God, I am living an idolatrous, unfulfilled life.

HOW EXPECTATION ELIMINATES THANK-FULNESS

Everybody wants what they can't have, you say. That's probably true.

In the first century, leprosy was something nobody wanted. A contagious skin disease that ate away flesh, leprosy exiled its victims from society—a separation from family, work, and worship. Even worse yet, the disease necessitated a total separation of the leper from any human touch. Lepers were required to shout "Unclean!" while they walked, so everyone else could maintain a safe distance from them. Instead of being able to hide the disability, lepers were commanded to openly announce their shame to everyone around them. All the time.

Imagine having to walk through life shouting, "Adulterer! Gossip! Workaholic! Porn addict! Chronically depressed!" Having to say it was nearly as horrible as having the disease itself.

Jesus knew that physical ailments also create spiritual and emotional ailments, so I'm not surprised that when Jesus healed lepers, He often placed His hands on them.[20] He welcomed them back into society with more than the words "Be healed." He reminded them of their worth as people, as His creation. He handed them freedom and value in exchange for enslavement and shame.

What might happen if someone were healed of this terrible disease? What if someone were given the one gift they wanted but never expected to have?

Consider the story of the ten lepers in Luke 17. As Jesus enters a little village on His way to Jerusalem, ten lepers call to him from a distance, "Jesus, Master, have mercy on us!"[21] They know Jesus is a healer and they hope to benefit from His power.

Jesus responds, "Go, show yourselves to the priests." Only the priest could declare a leper cleansed and free to return home. Jesus' command to go first requires that the lepers begin their journey in faith before they witness any change to their skin. Sure enough, while they walk towards the temple, their leprosy vanishes. Just what they had always dreamed about!

Yet only one man returns to thank Jesus. He runs back, praising God and falling on his knees in worship. To make the story even more dramatic, this man is a Samaritan, not a Jew. As an outcast and a foreigner, he occupies the lowest level of Jewish culture. In the Jewish mind, he deserved leprosy and anything else that happened to him.

> "Having more is not a sin but wanting more is. And it hooks us for life."

I've always wondered about the other nine lepers. Maybe Jesus felt puzzled, also, but most likely, He was making a point to the crowd when He asked, "Were not all ten cleansed? Where are the others? Was no one found to return and give praise except this foreigner?"[22]

Good question. Why weren't the nine lepers thankful? Perhaps they were just so excited to see their families that they forgot about Him? It's possible.

Call me a cynic, but I don't think people actually forget to say, "thank you." When we receive something and don't respond with thankfulness, it's because we either don't consider the gift valuable or we don't consider the giver valuable. When we are unthankful, we have probably arrived at the unconscious conclusion that the gift is deserved, or the giver is obligated to give; we smile politely and accept what we believe we should receive. If, however, someone lavishes an undeserved and extravagant gift on us, the words "thank you" will pour out automatically.

Thankfulness is a direct response to the perception and depth of need. I imagine that the Samaritan, being a foreigner, was well-acquainted with his insignificance in Jewish society, so he valued any act of grace.

Moses recorded God's perspectives on affluence and ungratefulness in a warning to the whining masses during the exodus: "For when you have eaten your fill, be sure to praise the Lord your God for the good land he has given you. But that is the time to be careful! Beware that in your plenty you do not forget the Lord your God and disobey his commands, regulations, and decrees that I am giving you today."[23]

We live in the good land. We have plenty. We are a chosen people. And when we pray, we tend to thank God mostly from a polite perspective. Not until we are aware of a deficit can we experience true gratefulness. Everything else we do is just good manners.

JUST SAY "THANK YOU"

As a parent, I talked about thankfulness nearly every day for more than 20 years. "Say *please* and *thank you*." "Use your manners." "Write a thank you note."

Why? There are a few good reasons. Being thankful is proper etiquette. It also proves to the general public that I'm not raising animals. Using manners is others-focused living, instead of self-focused living—it's the foundation for the battle against entitlement. Thankfulness is an irrepressible form of *soulspeak,* an effervescence in response to life.

Paul discusses the topic of joy and contentment to the church at Philippi in a letter he writes from prison. He knows that the church he has planted is experiencing great persecution and material want. He understands those needs firsthand, as he suffers himself from the cruel circumstances of confinement, abandonment, and neglect for the cause of Christ. To most people, it might seem like a good time to commiserate.

Yet Paul pens insightful perspectives about want and need. He doesn't just tell the Philippians to be thankful; he demonstrates it with his life. On a continuum of personal experience, he maps out the hills and valleys of a life spent focused on God's kingdom. Paul explains his transformation from wanting more, which comes from pride, to wanting nothing but Jesus, which comes from humility. Notices this paraphrase of Philippians 3:3-7 in *The Message:*

> "The very credentials these people are waving around as something special, I'm tearing up and throwing out with the trash—along with everything else I used to take credit for. And why? Because of Christ. Yes, all the things I once thought were so important are gone from my life. Compared to the high privilege of knowing Christ Jesus as my Master, firsthand, everything I once thought I had going for me is insignificant—dog dung. I've dumped it all in the trash so that I could embrace Christ and be embraced by him. I didn't want some petty, inferior brand of righteousness that comes from keeping a list of rules when I could get the robust kind that comes from trusting Christ—*God's* righteousness. I gave up all that inferior stuff so I could know Christ personally . . . I'm not saying that I have this all together, that I have it made. But I am well on my way, reaching out for Christ, who has so wondrously reached out for me. Friends, don't get me wrong: By no means do I count myself an expert in all of this, but I've got my eye on the goal, where God is beckoning us onward—to Jesus. I'm off and running, and I'm not turning back."[24]

Being thankful involves a process of emptying and refilling. Thankfulness is wakefulness to reality. It is an exchange of values, not a response to generosity, a natural outpouring of the attitudes of your soul.

LIVING IN TWO WORLDS

The gap between selfishness and contentment mirrors the expanse between the temporal and eternal. Paul explains, "Many live as enemies of the cross of Christ. Their destiny is destruction, their god is their stomach, and their glory is their shame. Their mind is on earthly things. But our citizenship is in heaven."[25] This epitomizes our culture; as much as we can *tsk-tsk* these pursuits, we are obsessed with the temporal world. In an effort to inhabit the world successfully, you and I often choose the wrong path ("their destiny is destruction"), feed the wrong appetites ("their god is their stomach"), and value the wrong activities ("their glory is their shame"). Maybe this little chart will help show the progression from values to behavior.

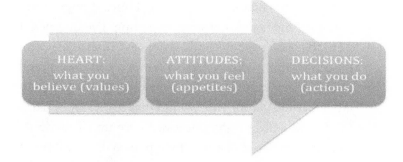

HEART: what you believe (values) — ATTITUDES: what you feel (appetites) — DECISIONS: what you do (actions)

Sin and faith habits both progress from the heart condition toward outward action. Wrong values (beliefs of the heart) develop wrong appetites (emotional and physical cravings); wrong appetites produce wrong actions (path toward destruction). No man in a healthy and loving marriage ever had an affair with his assistant the first time a lustful thought entered his head. An affair, like every other sin, is a destination—it's a destructive result of a pattern of actions (conversations, flirtations, pornography habit, isolation, shutting down emotionally at home, etc.), which result from a pattern of feeding appetites (pride, self-esteem, self-gratification, lust), which result from a value system (I deserve more; lust isn't wrong).

Because Jesus died on the cross to defeat the power of sin in our lives, our intentional continuation of sin patterns makes us direct enemies of all that Christ died for. Sin creates in us an unthankful, unappreciative, egocentric spirit. You make yourself Christ's enemy whenever you choose to sin. It's like pitching your tent in the enemy's camp and saying "I'd rather live here," even though Jesus has already died so you could camp with Him.

C. S. Lewis said, "We ought to give thanks for all fortune: if it is good, because it is good, if bad, because it works in us patience, humility and the contempt of this world and the hope of our eternal country."[26] Grace—accepting citizenship into a place we know we're not worthy of possessing—attacks pride and selfishness. It attacks the belief system that we will be happier with more and sadder with less. That true contentment can only come through worldly possessions. That God alone is not enough.

If we earn worthiness on our own, we will experience the pride that comes with self-attained success. And we won't be thankful. After all, you can't be thankful for something you've earned; you can only be proud of it. However, when we receive unmerited favor from the Lord, the accolades of this world will seem contemptible to us.

A TALE OF TWO FLOORS

Buying the wrong floor woke me up to a pride and greed problem. After two days of crying and mourning and apologizing to my husband for my many errors in judgment, Shane stepped in to solve the problem. He first called for professional advice from our friend George, who had contacts and experience regarding any household project. Shane explained what happened and asked how to correct the flooring problem.

George promptly sent out a contractor to rip up the red pine and install the white oak for us. He prepaid for everything. He was grace and generosity in the flesh.

We immediately responded with humility and thankfulness. The reality of being unworthy is decidedly uncomfortable, yet it's the exact environment where thanksgiving flourishes. The more we are aware of our deficit, the more thankful we will become.

PRAYER OF THANKSGIVING

Take a few seconds to pray David's prayer and notice *why* he's thankful. Then pray mine or form your own prayer of thanksgiving.

David's Prayer in Psalm 106:1-6:
Praise the Lord. Give thanks to the Lord for he is good; his love endures forever. Who can proclaim the mighty acts of the Lord or fully declare his praise? Blessed are they who maintain justice, who constantly do what is right. . . . We have sinned, even as our fathers did; we have done wrong and acted wickedly.

My prayer from Psalm 106:
Dear God of the heavens and the earth, you amaze me with your love. Thank you for your provision in my life. Even though I'm selfish, you provide over and above our needs. Thank you for taking care of me even when I doubt your love and protection. Thank you for forgiving my sins and redeeming my mistakes. I stand in awe of your love and mercy! Amen.

CHAPTER 10
CONTENT

THE QUEST FOR *more* leaks into every avenue of life. We can easily ignore or reinterpret the warning Paul gave his spiritual son Timothy: "Godliness with contentment is great gain."[27] Most of us want godliness—that's why we go to church—but I wonder if we're willing to become godly at the expense of being content with giving up gain.

The concept of gain carries spiritual ramifications as well. Does God bless us because we've been good boys and girls or because *He* is good? If God's blessing is an expression of His love, then blessing cannot be a reward for goodness. We cannot earn blessing by behaving well. And therefore, we cannot lose God's blessing by behaving poorly. God blesses us because of who He is, and His blessings cannot be interpreted through our understanding of what we want or need. Even pain can be a blessing because its purpose is to bring about transformation and worship, the two things that God desires most for us.

Blessings ought to remind us of our neediness, rather than encourage a spirit of expectation or entitlement. If we would remember that we are undeserving, we would live differently. Our lives become more about God and less about us. Herein hides the crux of a thankful spirit: thankfulness rises from a position of gratitude and destitution, not from affluence. It's a decidedly very un-Western perspective about gain and loss.

Thanksgiving, intrinsic to the faith process, ought to drive our prayers toward stronger faith. Thankfulness plays a critical role in guarding our hearts and minds against the enemy's lies. It is essential toward forming prayers that God answers.

Paul encouraged the Philippian church to view their trials from a humble position: "Do not be anxious about anything, but in everything, by prayer and petition, with thanksgiving, present your requests to God. And the peace of God, which transcends all understanding, will guard your hearts and your minds in Christ Jesus."[28] In defiance of human logic, Paul argued that thanksgiving builds a wall around gullible minds and defends us against the lies that we deserve more or that God doesn't care. Thankfulness frees us for powerful ministry.

Without being thankful, we just aren't capable of seeing our lives accurately. The temporal world is invading the battlefield of our understanding and subduing the eternal soul who lives there. Only strategized spiritual warfare can rout the enemy of selfishness and self-pity.

RESPONSE

While thankfulness resembles praise, they part company here. Praise is my grateful response for who God is, for His character and His person. Thankfulness is my grateful response for what God does, for His good deeds to an undeserved recipient. Praise reminds me of who God is, and thankfulness reminds me of what God does.

The words *thanks* or *thanksgiving* are used over 100 times in the Bible and appear in many repetitive phrases like these: "Give thanks to the Lord for he is good; his love endures forever"[29] and "Give thanks to the Lord for his unfailing love and his wonderful deeds for mankind."[30] In both imperatives, praise and thanksgiving are intertwined. Together, they provide an unstoppable force in transforming my misperceptions about God.

Below are reasons we should pray with thanksgiving; they come directly from the Psalms:

Why should we give thanks to God?

- Because He is good

- Because His love endures forever

Why does God deserve our thanks?

- For His unfailing love

- For His wonderful deeds for mankind

How should we give thanks to God?

- With praise (Ezra 3:11, Ps. 69:30, Ps. 100:4)

- When we pray (Eph. 1:16, 1 Tim. 2:1)

- When we're anxious (Phil 4:6)

- In every circumstance (1 Thess. 5:18, Col. 3:17)

- For everything (1 Tim. 4:4, Eph. 5:20)

- When we take communion (Mk. 8:6, Mtt. 26:27, Lk. 22:17, 1 Cor.11:24)

- When we eat (Jn. 6:11, 6:23, Acts 27:35)

UNDER PRESSURE

Thankfulness packs a powerful punch under pressure. When circumstances close in, and there's no exit in sight, being thankful will help you keep a level head and a level heart. I'm currently approaching my third birthday since I lost my mom to dementia. We share this birthday week, so as I approach my own birthday, I approach hers with a million shared memories. As the longing and grief begin to build, I am deciding this year to focus on thankfulness. I will remember, as much as possible, the myriad of things about my mother for which I am thankful, rather than dwelling on the myriad of things I miss about her. I am choosing not to look at the reality of today and instead focus on the countless blessings she sowed into my life.

Notice that Daniel did a similar thing. In Daniel 6, prior to his historic and miraculous survival in a lions' den, we see him in the habit of giving thanks during his prayers. His regular meetings with God prepare his heart against despair and give his prayers power against his enemies—people or animals. He is already focusing on what God has done and what God will do when the reality of the lions' den comes into view.

As the premiere counselor to the king (and a captive at that), Daniel becomes the nemesis of King Darius' jealous counselors. When Darius the Mede conquered the Babylonian empire, he acquired the Babylonian wise men from King Belshazzar, including the renowned Daniel. I can't imagine the Medo-Persian wisemen liked him much.

Jealous and intent on orchestrating Daniel's downfall, Darius' counselors search for a reason to vilify him. All they can find is an unwavering habit of praying while he faces west toward Jerusalem, three times each day. The counselors persuade Darius to outlaw worship to anyone but himself.

Daniel's response under duress reflects his character, as does yours and mine. "When Daniel learned that the decree had been published, he went home to his upstairs room where the windows opened toward Jerusalem. Three times a day he got down on his knees and prayed, giving thanks to God, just as he had done before."[31]

Giving thanks to God! Daniel knew the edict and the punishment for disobeying it, yet he had already purposed in his heart to follow God for his entire life. His prayers of thanksgiving were protecting his heart from doubting what he believed about God. His faith held up under pressure.

THANKFUL AND BRAVE

Several years ago, a godly woman in my church named Courtney was diagnosed with Stage 4 melanoma. She bravely underwent surgery, chemotherapy, radiation, and drug trials.

She helped her daughter plan a wedding and enjoyed her first grandchild's birth. She continued faithfully attending church, always wearing a smile and a beautiful headscarf. I wondered how she could keep up such a brave front under the prospect of leaving behind her adoring husband and four lovely daughters. I surmised that she fell apart at home. Who wouldn't?

One day, I asked her husband Bill how she was doing *for real*. He told me Courtney's secret for living with joy and determination: every morning, she woke with a smile and quoted Psalm 118:24—"This is the day that the Lord has made. We will rejoice and be glad in it."

Courtney had determined to be thankful for each of her days, right up until the end. After a year of bravely fighting the cancer, she passed away. Bill was able to smile through her funeral and give praise to the Lord for their life together because like Daniel, they had practiced a culture of thankfulness in their marriage. They lived with an eternal perspective that even death and disappointed hopes would not crush.

Perhaps thanksgiving brings about emotional and spiritual triumphs because it counteracts grief. Sorrow drowns in the present and longs for the past, but thanksgiving looks forward with hope and faith.

Psalm 118 begins and ends with, "Give thanks unto the Lord for he is good; his love endures forever." The second clause continues to appear throughout the song as a refrain, providing the psalm's theme. Buried in the *soulspeak* of this song are the reasons to be thankful:

- "In my anguish I cried to the Lord, and he answered by setting me free. The Lord is with me; I will not be afraid. What can man do to me?" (vv. 5-6)

- "It is better to take refuge in the Lord than to trust in man." (v. 8)

- "I was pushed back and about to fall, but the Lord helped me. The Lord is my strength and my song; he has become my salvation." (v. 13)

- "This is the gate of the Lord through which the righteous may enter. I will give you thanks, for you have answered me; you have become my salvation." (vv. 20-21)

- "You are my God, and I will give you thanks. You are my God, and I will exalt you." (v. 28)

CUTTING AWAY THE ENSLAVEMENT

If you want to become a truly thankful person, you must intentionally create a thankful heart. This part will hurt a little because it's a process that moves you toward thankfulness. You must cut away the selfishness that lives naturally inside of you, and you must replace the selfishness with humility. That's right. The opposite of selfishness is not exactly generosity. More accurately, it's humility.

We all give when it benefits us. Humility, however, prompts pure sacrifice. As demonstrated through Jesus' sacrifice on the cross, humility produces generosity without any personal expectation or reciprocity attached to it. "Your attitude should be the same as that of Christ Jesus . . . he humbled himself and became obedient to death—even death on a cross!"[32] True humility deprives itself of its rights and offers up itself to the undeserving.

Here's a chart to show how humility (specifically thankfulness) can transform a life:

THE PUT OFF/PUT ON PRINCIPLE (EPH. 4) TO CREATE A THANKFUL HEART

Put off discontentment	Put on thankfulness	Scripture
Greed & Materialism	Give away your things and don't replace them; speak grateful words about your material things; fast from buying new things	Phil 4:16-19; Luke 12:15; Ecc. 5:10-11; Mtt. 6:2-4; Rom. 13:7; 2 Cor. 9:6-7; Acts 20:35; Mtt. 6:19-21, 33-34
Stealing	Give back what you've stolen; give away your won things	Ex. 20;15; Eph. 4:28; Lev. 19:13; Prov. 10:2
Complaining	Speak praise; stop critiquing everything	1 Cor. 10:10; Phil. 2:14-16; Jude 16; Jms. 3:5-6
Jealousy & Envy	Compliment others and thank God for your blessings	Ex. 20:17; Rom. 12:15; Prov. 14:30; 2 Cor. 12:20; Jms. 4:1-2
Discontentment	Serve people who are truly needy; give to people in need	Phil. 4:12; 1 Tim. 6:6-8; Heb. 13:5; Ecc. 4:8

Tips to help you become thankful:

- Make a list of the blessings in your life and thank God for them
- Pray a blessing over the person you're jealous of
- Give away things you value
- Volunteer at a homeless shelter or soup kitchen
- Buy things for other people and give them away anonymously

- Keep a prayer journal
- List God's blessings when you pray
- Go on a mission trip
- When you have a complaint, write it down and find a blessing to counteract it

REVIEW OF THANKSGIVING:

- Be thankful for who God is and for what He does
- A thankful spirit comes from humility
- Wanting *more* will enslave you into thanklessness, regardless of what you get
- Being thankful is a carefully groomed habit that will keep you from despair
- In order to be thankful, you must replace your selfishness with humble generosity

PRAYER OF THANKSGIVING

We have so much to be thankful for! Give these two prayers a whirl.

David's prayer from Psalm 7:17:
I will give thanks to the Lord because of his righteousness; I will sing the praises of the name of the Lord Most High.

My prayer from Psalm 7:17:
Lord, thank you for being holy, right, and good. I praise You because I am confident that You always do good for me and can only do good. Thank you for the many blessings in my life. You are the Lord of everything, and I worship You. Amen.

PART 6:
"PRETTY PLEASE":
SPEAKING REQUESTS

I call on you, O God, for you will answer me;
Give ear to me and hear my prayer.
Show the wonder of your great love,
You who save by your right hand
those who take refuge in you from their foes.
Keep me as the apple of your eye;
Hide me in the shadow of your wings
from the wicked who assail me,
from my mortal enemies who surround me.
And I—in righteousness I will see your face;
When I awake, I will be satisfied with seeing your likeness.
Psalm 17:6-9, 15

CHAPTER 11
POWERLESS

WE WERE IN Sedona, AZ for spring break, 2009. Our boys were ages fifteen, thirteen, and eight and having the vacation of a lifetime. When you've lived your whole life in the Midwest and East Coast, nothing energizes your adventuring spirit like tramping through the changing colors of a great red rocks desert. After a few days hiking and climbing in the Verde Valley of Sedona, we set off on the week's biggest adventure: the Grand Canyon.

We woke the boys before dawn. Our backpacks were already stocked with water bottles, granola bars, fruit, and peanut butter-and-jelly sandwiches. We were dressed in layers. Although Sedona's temperature would hit the low 80s that day, the Grand Canyon would be 35 degrees at the top. We would shed layers as we descended through the canyon.

My goal, as the cautious matron of our family, was to hike with my husband and children halfway down the canyon on the Kaibab Trail, then go back up in time to catch the sun setting over the multicolored layers. (I never miss a sunset.) We only had one day here, so we needed to make it count. We would drive back to Sedona after dark.

My husband had his heart set on hiking the whole canyon in one day because he remembered doing it as a kid. I was skeptical. I had read all the guidebooks, which made me aware of the physical toll hiking the whole canyon could take on a person. All guidebooks recommended either hiking partway or camping at the bottom and hiking back up one-two days later. Since we already had a condo paid for in Sedona, spending a night at the bottom of the canyon didn't seem like a logical option. We would just hike as far as we could in one day, making sure we returned to the top before sunset.

We arrived and surveyed the canyon in all its morning glory. My eyes welled up with tears. I whispered, "Wow! Look what God made!" Then mom-mode kicked in, and I said, "I can't believe they don't have guard rails around the edge. Someone could fall right off and die!"

Apparently, people have. The gift shop was awash with books telling the stories of a thousand accidental deaths—from falling off, backing off, dying of exposure, rattlesnake bites, helicopter crashes, rafting mishaps, rock-climbing falls, hang-gliding accidents, ballooning accidents, and plane crashes. At the welcome center, Shane caught me frantically skimming a book. "Put it down. We're just walking. We'll be fine."

The rangers also emphasized the danger. "Do not attempt to hike the canyon in one day. Many have died or been hospitalized trying this. The canyon is much more strenuous than it looks. Its elevation is 5,000 feet. Please take a lot of water . . ."

My eyes were saucers by this point. Shane shook his head at me. *It might be hard for some people, but not us,* his look told me. After all, he had completed an Ironman competition that year, our oldest son ran cross-country for his high school, and our other boys played travel soccer. I've even been known to exercise on occasion. We would be fine.

Of course, we'd be fine. We were prepared, and we were only hiking half of it.

By the time we began our hike, it was already 11:00 a.m. We would need to hurry. The steep Kaibab Trail unwound below us, careening around tight corners and over the rocky surface. I took a billion pictures. The panorama was majestic.

I did notice warning signs along the way about being careful of edges and exertion, but I no longer worried; the canyon had captured me. I felt like a true adventurer.

We began shedding our outer layers as we walked. First, off came the hats and gloves, then the coats. Then sweatshirts. At the halfway point, we were down to shorts and T-shirts. We ate lunch in the shade of a boulder; we had been hydrating regularly, and we felt great.

"I think we can do the whole thing," said Shane. "We've got enough food and water. We feel good."

"I don't think there's going to be enough daylight left. And going up will be a lot slower," I said.

"Okay, let's take the Angel Trail back up. It's longer, but less steep, and it's lit. There are water stations along the way. We can also refill our bottles at the ranch at the bottom."

Bruce, our high-schooler, was game for the adventure.

"Brady and I will never make it," I said, looking at my eight-year-old and calculating the time on my watch.

"I'll stay with Mom, too," said Brent. "I don't want to hike that far."

It was settled. Shane and Bruce would hike the rest at a faster pace, and we would go back up and watch the sunset. We transferred some supplies to their backpack and parted ways after a gorgeous family photo at the edge. The canyon's purple-and-orange layers streaked behind us. The sky sparkled bright blue.

Perfect.

We began our ascent, which proved much more challenging than anticipated, while Shane and Bruce raced down the trail to the bottom, stopping to text whenever they had reception. They made it to the ranch in good time. They refreshed their water and snacks. Everything was fine. They felt exhilarated.

We heard nothing from Shane for a few hours. As we watched the sunset paint the canyon in splendid shades, they hiked somewhere, thousands of feet below us. I took the boys to a gift shop and then a restaurant, where we filled up on cafeteria food.

Then I got a scratchy call from Shane. I walked outside to listen. "Hey! How are you? Where are you? We've already eaten dinner," I said.

"Honey, you need to pray." His voice sounded strained and serious.

"Why? What happened?"

"It's Bruce. He's—he's not good."

"What do you mean?" The pit of my stomach lurched violently.

"We might have to go back down—spend the night down here—rent a tent. Bruce might not make it back up."

"What do you mean 'not make it'?" My mouth went dry.

"He's gassed. We've been hydrating here and sitting for a long time, waiting for him to acclimate."

"What's wrong with him?"

"I didn't know—I didn't realize—" His voice broke. I waited. "It's the altitude. We've covered too much altitude in too short a time. Going fast turns out to have been the wrong approach."

Edema! I should have thought of it. Having taught middle school English (not to mention being a boy-mom), I had read my share of stories about mountain climbers on Everest and K2. My brother was also a mountain climber, and he had talked about pulmonary edema (mountain sickness) many times.

The greatest danger to hikers, even on an easy mountain, is ascending too quickly. A hiker's blood must adapt gradually to the oxygen change or his lungs will begin filling with fluid, causing swelling, difficulty breathing, dehydration, exhaustion, and disorientation. Without a quick descent to a lower altitude, hikers with edema can die. The same danger exists for deep-sea divers, whose descent into the ocean depths must be handled gradually so their lungs can adjust.

Shane and Bruce had descended and ascended thousands of feet in several hours, and none of it was at an elevation where they typically exercised.

"Then go back down," I said. "Don't risk it. What should I do? We don't have anywhere to spend the night. I'm sure the hotels are full."

"I don't know. I'll call again if I get cell coverage. Oh, wait. He's starting to perk up. Maybe we can still make it. We are more than halfway up. It's so far to go back down to the bottom and then try to find a place to stay. We might give it one more try."

I prayed hard, laying out earnest requests and lamenting to the Lord. Certainly, God wouldn't hold our mistake against us, would He?

An hour later, I received a fuzzy call. "Honey ..." Shane's voice was cracking. I could tell he was holding back tears. "I don't think we can make it—I've been trying to carry him on my back."

Panic seized me. I could picture my husband, stooped over, with a boy taller than he hung over his shoulders. "He's not better?"

"He's throwing up. He's delusional. No one is around. The trail is completely empty—I know it's not that far—" His voice cracked again. "Just pray! We need a miracle! I'm trying to take him back down, if I can hold out. It's just so far, and I think it might be too late—"

We lost the signal.

I left the boys in the restaurant and went out to the car and sat in the driver's seat, sobbing under an endless canopy of stars. I cried out in lamentation. I pleaded with God from the depths of my heart. My *soulspeak* rose to heaven in raw agony as I made the biggest request of my life. "Save my son, God! Oh, don't let him die because we were foolish! We didn't know! Oh, God, how could this happen?"

I returned to the restaurant, ashen-faced. I told the boys that Bruce wasn't feeling well, and we all prayed together.

Another hour crawled by, while my heart hammered in my chest. Then I got a call. "We made it. Which restaurant are you in?"

I began to sob. In a matter of a few minutes, they arrived. Bruce looked tired, but he smiled and let me enfold him in my arms and cry on his shoulder. He inhaled his dinner and went back for seconds. Shane was haggard. I waited until he had finished eating before I questioned him.

"What happened?" I asked. "He doesn't look too bad."

He shook his head. "It was a miracle. A real miracle."

We all listened attentively, including Bruce. He couldn't re-member any of the ascent.

Shane told us how he had hoisted Bruce on his back, car-rying him until his own body screamed for rest. Bruce couldn't stand up, let alone walk, and his legs had turned completely blue. He couldn't focus or speak. His eyes had glazed over, and he had vomited everything he'd ingested that day. They had no more water and saw no water refilling stations anywhere.

At 9:00 p.m., the Angel Trail was empty as far as they could see in both directions. Shane had no cell reception—no way to call 911 or me or the park service. He was alone with our son, and he had nothing that could help him. They were descend-ing toward the ranch, miles below them in the darkness.

A port-a-potty sat slightly off the trail. Shane carried him to it so Bruce could hang his head over the potty. He was still vomiting, although his stomach was empty. Shane closed the door and paced in front of it, praying.

A woman suddenly appeared on the main trail behind them, seemingly from the path below, although Shane had not noticed anyone climbing toward them. Her headlamp bobbed against the night sky as she walked toward him. She wore hiking clothes and had a backpack and a red fanny pack strapped around her waist. She was elderly but strong. She wasn't winded, even though she must have come up fast. Shane wondered how he could have missed the light of her headlamp in the darkness.

"You in trouble?" she asked.

"Yes," Shane responded. "My son's inside, throwing up. My family's waiting up top, but I'm trying to take him back down. He can't even walk."

"What's wrong with him?"

"He's thrown up everything he's eaten or drunk today. His legs are blue. He's dizzy and disoriented. I've been carrying him." He couldn't keep his voice from breaking.

"Edema," she said briskly. She unzipped the fanny pack and pulled out a little white tablet. "Here, put this under his tongue. He needs to drink this entire bottle of water." She pulled out a plastic water bottle, surprisingly cold. "The entire bottle."

Shane studied her in the shadows, in her army green clothes and her messy white hair. He had no idea what this tablet was, but he took it from her hand and opened the door to the port-a-potty. "Buddy, you gotta take this."

Bruce was sitting on the dirty floor, dazed. Shane opened Bruce's mouth and placed the pill under his tongue. He put the water bottle in Bruce's hand and helped him raise it and begin drinking. Bruce swallowed the pill with his first sip and began guzzling the water. Shane waited, eyes glued on him.

A minute later, Bruce tried to stand. Shane pulled him to his feet, studying him.

"You okay? Think you can walk a little?"

Bruce nodded. They exited the port-a-potty, and Shane looked for the woman so he could thank her again.

Angel Trail was empty, above and below them, and Bruce had already begun walking quickly up the canyon trail. Shane looked for the woman's lamplight in every direction, hoping to catch her as he raced up the trail after Bruce.

"You never saw her again?"

Shane shook his head. "I looked for her all the way up. No way could she have gotten up faster than us. I could barely catch up to Bruce. *He was running full speed.*"

Chills ran down my back and arms. She had to be an angel, on Angel Trail.

UNTIL WE'RE POWERLESS

That crisis on Angel Trail reinforced several truths to our family about faith. Foremost, it reminded us how powerful God is and how much He loves us. Secondly, it reminded us how little we access His power over our lives. Not until we feel utterly and completely helpless, do we assault God's throne in fervent prayer. Until danger appears, like it did at the Grand Canyon, we assume we have the knowledge, skill, and supplies to carry out our own plans. It often takes a tragedy or trauma for us to realize how desperately we must rely on God and how much we need to pray.

If there's one question surrounding the theology of prayer requests, it's probably "How do I get an answer?" (More specifically, "How do I get a *yes*?") When we're praying for a job, safety, deliverance, or material needs, we are certainly looking for clear wisdom and direction—some supernatural detour that leads us swiftly and obviously toward the best choice, with as little waiting as possible. But A. W. Pink observes,

> "The prevailing idea seems to be, that I come to God and ask Him for something that I want, and that I expect Him to give me that which I have asked. But this is a most dishonoring and degrading conception. The pop-

ular belief reduces God to a servant, our servant: doing our bidding, performing our pleasure, granting our desires."[33]

Okay, but doesn't God want to give us the desires of our hearts? Psalm 20:4 says, "May he give you the desire of your heart and make all your plans succeed." That's all we're asking for. Success and happiness. Psalm 37:4 clarifies the promise a little more: "Take delight in the Lord, and he will give you the desires of your heart." *Take delight in the Lord*. You know what *delight* is? Delight is the expression on new parents' faces when their baby smiles at them, coos at them, or says "Dada" on cue. Delight is pure revelry. It demands nothing.

DOES GOD WANT TO ANSWER MY RE-QUESTS?

Many of us operate like God has a limited number of prayer requests to grant, so we need to get in line and grab a ticket, like we're standing in a group of impatient shoppers at the deli counter. We try not to overdo it, in case God gets annoyed and puts a hold on the whole request-answering system.

Here's a truth that might blow your mind: You can't ask God for too much. God *wants* to answer your requests. He never gets sick of you. You don't bother Him when you call Him up. Yes, He knows everything, but He still wants you to ask.

God responds to our requests with delight. Scriptures contain countless phrases describing God's desire to hear our prayers and answer them. Consider the following promises:

- "May the Lord grant all your requests." (Ps. 20:5)
- "You have granted him his heart's desire and have not withheld the request of his lips." (Ps. 21:2)
- "And when he prayed to him, the Lord was moved by his entreaty and listened to his plea." (2 Chron. 33:13)

- "I call on you, my God, for you will answer me; turn your ear to me and hear my prayer." (Psalm 17:6)
- "'Call to me and I will answer you and tell you great and unsearchable things you do not know.'" (Jer. 33:3)

As of now, two of our sons have graduated from college. When each of them left home as freshmen, they couldn't wait to spread their wings and experience some independence. They were excited to set their own schedules and make their own decisions apart from our watchful eyes. They were fairly confident they could handle the future.

We waited on pins and needles. When would they call? When would they want to come home to visit? We'd get brief texts like "I'm fine," "Can you put some money in my account?" or "I need you to send . . ."

Not the communication we were looking for, although we were still happy to hear from them. Over time, their communication increased, but they could still go for stretches without checking in. Were we upset?

> "You can't ask God for too much. God wants to answer your requests."

No. We knew our children loved us. We knew they loved being with us. They were just adapting to a stage in life that took all their concentration and emotional energy. We didn't hold that against them; we understood because we remembered what it felt like to be in college, learning how to become an adult.

Yet we still longed to hear from them. We delighted in their company and conversation whenever we could get it. We also loved meeting their needs.

When they called (and they did), just to chat—our world would stop. Nothing else mattered more. The boys might begin with great news, like an A paper or a positive comment from their coaches, or they might just go straight into sharing a recent disappointment. They might ask for our advice. Sometimes, I suspected they called just to hear our voices. We leaped to respond to requests that came from relational interactions.

Just like we parents love to have these conversations with our children, God craves conversation with us. When He hears our *soulspeak*, He leaps to answer. He cherishes the intimacy that our requests bring.

When you are present in a loving relationship with your Heavenly Father, you can expect an eager response from Him. It's the whole reason He created us. He's God the Father. He wants to give. It's his nature to give. Jesus promises,

> "Ask and it will be given to you; seek and you will find; knock and the door will be opened to you. For everyone who asks receives; the one who seeks finds; and to the one who knocks, the door will be opened. Which of you, if your son asks for bread, will give him a stone? Or if he asks for a fish, will give him a snake? If you, then, though you are evil, know how to give good gifts to your children, how much more will your Father in heaven give good gifts to those who ask Him!"[34]

How about a sigh of relief? God wants to answer your requests.

Read this prayer from Moses and then try praying my adaptation.

PRAYER OF REQUEST

I know you know how to ask for stuff. We're all good at that. But take note of how Moses talks to God and what he asks for. Then pray these prayers or form your own.

Moses' prayer in Exodus 33:12-16:
If you are pleased with me, teach me your ways so I may know you and continue to find favor with you. Remember that this nation is your people…. If your Presence does not go with us,

do not send us up from here. How will anyone know that you are pleased with me and with your people unless you go with us? What else will distinguish me and your people from all the other people on the face of the earth? . . . Now show me your glory.

My prayer from Exodus 33:
Oh, Lord, God of all creation, I sit in awe of You! You have called me for a purpose, and I am overwhelmed by it. I cannot do anything You ask of me unless You go with me and before me. Thank You for using me. Make me a useful vessel, and keep me remembering that I am never worthy of Your love, no matter what I do or who I become. You alone are worthy of all glory, honor, and praise. I just ask for Your blessing and Your spirit to reside in me. Show me your glory! Reflect your glory through me, so that when people see my life, they only see You! Amen.

CHAPTER 12
CLEAN HANDS, PURE HEARTS

WILL GOD REALLY answer *all* our prayers?

That depends on how we look at it. We might refuse to accept the answer given. We might not wait long enough to hear the answer. We might spend time negotiating for a better answer. But God will always answer. He's promised.

We're good at keeping ourselves acutely aware of decision deadlines and itinerary timetables. We expect God to keep up with our demands if He wants to be worshipped. We're on a tight schedule here on earth, so time is of the essence.

The Bible speaks a good bit about why we don't get our prayers answered. God gives several reasons for this:

- "If I had cherished sin in my heart, the Lord would not have listened." (Ps. 66:18)
- "Husbands, in the same way be considerate as you live with your wives and treat them with respect as the weaker partner and as heirs with you of the gracious gift of life, so that nothing will hinder your prayers." (1 Pet. 3:7)
- "When Saul saw the Philistine army, he was afraid; terror filled his heart. He inquired of the Lord, but the Lord did not answer him . . . Saul then said to his attendants, 'Find me a woman who is a medium, so I may go and inquire of her.'" (I Sam. 28:5-7)

Not hearing from God can drive a person to foolish and destructive decisions. Consider the last reference above, about King Saul. When he couldn't get a response from God, he resorted to his spiritual enemy, the Devil (through a witch's power). This last recourse came from Saul's lifelong pattern of making his own decisions based on his insecurity, instead of a heart conformed to God's will. Instead of receiving God's blessing and direction in his life, his bondage to insecurity cost him his life, his son's life, and his kingdom. Saul's self-reliance had enslaved him.

> "Please remember: it is always God's will for you to be free from strongholds. As stated . . . we may not always be sure God will heal us physically in this life of every disease or prosper us with tangible blessings, but He always wills to free us from strongholds. You will never have to worry about whether you are praying in God's will concerning strongholds. 'It is for freedom that Christ has set us free.'"[35]

As long as we're in a pattern of confession, we can remain confident in the power of our requests.

WHAT IS MY RESPONSIBILITY WHEN I ASK FOR SOMETHING?

Yep, making a request requires some skin in the game. You have some responsibility when you invite God's participation.

Consider this. How do you want to be approached when someone asks a favor of you? Arrogant, assuming, or demanding? Insecure, groveling, or disbelieving? I'll bet their attitude affects your reaction and response.

When you approach God, what is your posture? Do you doubt He wants to help? Are you angry, embarrassed, or afraid to ask for help? The attitude behind your approach reveals your perception of God's character.

Paul instructs his church in Thessalonica to "Give thanks in all circumstances; for this is God's will for you in Christ Jesus."[36] Every previous pattern of prayer we've discussed prepares you to make powerful requests. But if you don't have a heart that's pure enough to implore God to act on your behalf, your requests will seem "unanswered" by the One who promises to give you the desires of your heart.

David describes the person who has God's attention like this:

> "Who may ascend the mountain of the Lord?
> Who may stand in his holy place?
> The one who has clean hands and a pure heart,
> Who does not trust in an idol or swear by a false god.
> They will receive blessing from the Lord
> And vindication from God their Savior."[37]

What does vindication mean, and why is that a good thing? *Vindication* means "justified." In other words, if you want God to listen and respond to you, you should consistently have:

- clean hands (right actions)
- a pure heart (right motivation)
- no trust in idols (right values)

Those who aspire to this calling move the heart of God. None of us have clean hands, pure hearts, and worshipful attitudes all the time. Probably not even a fraction of the time. Don't panic. Once again, God knows our hearts, and He sees the difference between those striving and failing and those failing because they aren't striving or don't care. The people who move God pray boldly, specifically, and regularly.

CAN I TRUST GOD'S ANSWERS?

When you're waiting for an answer or you don't like the answer you've gotten, you must remember what God says: "'My thoughts are nothing like your thoughts... And my ways are far beyond anything you could imagine.'"[38] He has eternal perspective for the souls of mankind. You and I would prefer to choose answers for ourselves or give God the plan we'd like Him to execute. But if you truly believe that God is good and He only does good, you must choose faith. You must believe that God will respond to your pleas according to His perfect will.

This is how we know God is trustworthy:

- "You may ask me for anything in my name, and I will do it." (Jn. 14:14)
- "Now to him who is able to do immeasurably more than all we ask or imagine, according to his power that is at work within us, to him be glory in the church and in Christ Jesus throughout all generations, for ever and ever! Amen." (Eph. 3:20-21)
- "The thief comes only to steal and kill and destroy; I have come that they may have life, and have it to the full." (Jn. 10:10)
- "And to know this love that surpasses knowledge— that you may be filled to the measure of all the fullness of God. Now to him who is able to do immeasurably more than all we ask or imagine, according to his power that is at work within us, to him be glory in the church and in Christ Jesus throughout all generations, for ever and ever! Amen." (Eph. 3:19-21)

We also have a Bible filled with stories of God's faithfulness because God knows that it takes us humans a lot to trust.

EMBARRASSED

In my Minnesota community, I grew up in a Christian home, Christian church, and Christian school. A Christian bubble, really, where everyone knew how to behave and why to behave, and we gave God the glory for all the good things that happened.

God came in handy during a crisis. Enter the Wednesday night prayer meeting, designed for both the mundane and the miracle-needing prayer requests. Whether for job interviews, cancer, or missionaries in Africa, Wednesday night provided the venue for bigger prayers to operate. The really important and dramatic requests, called *unspokens*, were shared here. Whenever someone needed prayer for something particularly personal, they would ask you to pray for their *unspoken* request.

In hindsight, the *unspokens* comprised the whole purpose for prayer meeting. Instead of casually mentioning "all the *unspokens*," perhaps we ought to have prayed for the real issues themselves—the failing marriages and rebellious children and shattered faith.

Unspoken requests require real prayer from real warrior prayers—facedown, tearful entreaties backed by absolute reassurance that God cares and will respond. But instead, these needs got a quick once-over. Why? Because we were embarrassed about the real areas of need in our lives. We were more concerned about looking perfect than becoming perfect.

Here's where requests might overlap with intercession. Sometimes, my requests weigh so heavily on my heart that I must employ the prayers of others to intercede for my burdens. More on that in Part 7.

> "Prayer warriors aren't perfect. They just pray out of desperation."

FORMULA FOR REQUESTS

You want a formula for powerful prayer. Of course, you do. I do too.

But there is no formula for the perfect request, the one that will annihilate your enemy and elicit a *yes* response from the Creator of the universe. Prayer is ultimately and only about a relationship. Since you can't trick an omniscient God into believing you love Him any more than you actually do, you will have to begin with praise before you can pray any other way. In worship, you must adore God for who He is and make peace with His sovereign will for you, however that might look. Then you must confess your sin so your heart is pure. You might pour out some laments to understand the heart of God. You should thank Him for the blessings you already enjoy, because that gives you perspective on your current requests. Then you ask for His will, and He reveals it to you.

This isn't a formula, but these are components present in the prayers of the greatest prayer warriors in the Bible, people who praised, confessed, lamented, and thanked *before* they asked.

Then lives were saved, enemies were exposed, armies failed, miracles occurred, and the enemies of God were vanquished. Everyday stuff in the life of a prayer warrior.

THE BLESSING OF IMPERFECTION

But what if you're not that spiritual? What if you doubt that you can do this?

Even better.

This is how you will rely on God's power. When the father in Mark 9 came to Jesus and begged Him to cast out the demon that tormented his son, Jesus responded, "All things are possible to him who believes." Immediately, "the father of the child cried out and said, 'I believe; help my unbelief.'"[39] He admitted wanting to believe but finding it difficult. Consider some regular people in the Bible who learned to pray with power as they learned to believe.

Take Moses, who stuttered so terribly he needed Aaron to talk for him. Esther, a frightened girl, was yanked from her home and placed into the king's harem to be raped as part of her "job interview" for queen. Gideon tested God's will for his life by putting out a fleece and asking for the morning dew to fall or not fall on it. Hezekiah tested God's answer by asking Him to reverse shadows on a stairway.

Even Elijah suffered from fear and exhaustion. After calling down fire from heaven, he ran into the wilderness to escape from Jezebel; God nourished him and then instructed him to anoint Elisha as his replacement. After being a spiritual leader for his subjects, David stole Bathsheba from her husband Uriah and had Uriah killed to cover up the affair; the baby they had died, and David's adult children repeated his sins of sexual assault and murder.

People can be incredible prayer warriors one minute and desperate sinners the next. Somehow, God sees past human frailties, into the heart, and He decides—for whatever reason—that He wants to bless us and use us when we approach His throne with clean hands and pure hearts and *just ask for His help*.

Prayer warriors aren't perfect. They just pray out of desperation. They believe.

REVIEW OF REQUESTS

- God wants to answer your requests
- Come before God helpless, in an attitude of worship, with sin confessed and a thankful spirit
- Pray in faith; trust that His will is best

- Pray in a group; share your requests with others so they can pray for you

- Be helpless before God so He can show Himself mighty on your behalf

Read the samples below of requests. Notice the incorporation of the previous types of prayer: praise, confession, lamentation, and thanksgiving!

PRAYER OF REQUEST

When you get a chance, read the story of Hezekiah in 2 Kings 16-19, 2 Chronicles 28-32, and Isaiah 36-38. The man's prayers got results! Also, read through these prayers and pray them.

Hezekiah's prayer in 2 Kings 19:15-19:
O Lord, God of Israel, enthroned between the cherubim, you alone are God over all the kingdoms of earth. You have made heaven and earth. Give ear, O Lord, and hear; open your eyes, O Lord, and see … Now, O Lord our God, deliver us … so that all kingdoms on earth may know that you alone, O Lord, are God.

My prayer from 2 Kings 19:
Dear Lord, the Maker of heaven and earth! I am amazed at Your glory and power. We need Your power at work in our world. I know You can defeat the enemy of this world that tells us lies. Deliver and protect my kids. Make me vigilant and courageous. Help us testify of Your love and greatness. Amen.

PART 7: "SOMEONE NEEDS HELP": SPEAKING INTERCESSION

Now if You slay this people as one man,
then the nations who have heard of Your fame will say,
"Because the LORD could not bring this people into the land
which He promised them by oath,
therefore He slaughtered them in the wilderness."
But now, I pray, let the power of the Lord be great, just as
You have declared,
"The LORD is slow to anger and abundant in lovingkindness,
forgiving iniquity and transgression;
but He will by no means clear the guilty, visiting the iniquity of the fathers on the children to the third and the fourth
generations."
Pardon, I pray, the iniquity of this people
according to the greatness of Your lovingkindness,
just as You also have forgiven this people, from Egypt even
until now.
Numbers 14:15-19

CHAPTER 13
HELLO?

CRYSTAL, A YOUNG *woman who led worship in our college ministry at Virginia Commonwealth University, was driving her car, with her baby boy Caleb strapped behind her in his infant car seat.*

A massive, soundless collision shattered glass in slow motion, spraying shards into the car, crumpling metal like wrapping paper. The airbag deployed into Crystal's face while her body lurched forwards. The seat belt snagged her and slammed her back into her seat. Baby Caleb lunged up in his infant seat, his newborn head rocking violently, while the little straps dug into his neck. An ambulance arrived, and paramedics quickly cut Crystal out of the front seat and hovered over her. Resuscitation began over the lifeless infant.

That's when Shane awoke, panting and sweating, searching his surroundings for clues of time and place. He took deep breaths to slow his pulse. The clock read 3:05 a.m. Picking up his cell phone from the nightstand, he searched his call history. No one had called him. He considered the logic of Crystal being out at 3 a.m. with Caleb. Not likely. But something was not right . . .

Shane said a prayer over Crystal's family and tried to go back to sleep. The dream continued hanging raw in his mind, so he slid out of bed and went down to the living room, where he knelt and prayed for two hours over Crystal's family. When the heaviness finally lifted, he went back up to bed and fell fitfully to sleep.

In the morning, as Shane left for work, he said to me, "Can you call Crystal this morning and check on her? I had a horrible dream about her and Caleb last night. Except it didn't feel like a normal dream where things aren't logical—it was super clear, like a movie." He then told me about the dream.

I phoned soon after. "Hello? How are you guys today? Everybody okay?"

Crystal sounded a bit tired. "Well, Caleb is teething, so we were up a good bit last night. He's running a low fever."

I felt relieved but confused. I didn't tell her about Shane's dream. Maybe we were too naïve about how this intercession stuff worked. "Oh, well, let me know if you need anything." I said good-bye and hung up. Then I called Shane and gave him the report.

"Huh," he said. "I wonder what that dream was about."

We both ran our normal daily routine. Then at 4 p.m., my phone rang. "Hello?" My pulse quickened.

"Did you hear about Crystal?" a girl from our college group asked me.

My heart sank right into my shoes. "No, what happened?"

"She and Caleb were in a car accident today. The car is totaled. The ambulance came and took them to the hospital, but they're fine. They're at home now."

I sank into a chair and cried. My husband, in blind faith, had waged spiritual warfare over a young family and won. His intercession had changed the course of their lives and the lives of their loved ones.

SILLY MANTRA OR ESSENTIAL PRACTICE?

Until this point in my life, I had spent a good bit of my prayer time focused on the previous five types of prayers: praise, confession, lament, thanksgiving, and requests (mostly requests, let's be honest) for our family and ministry needs. I believed that God answered prayers and that His will was sovereign.

Although I prayed out of obedience and conviction, I assumed God had everything handled and that my responsibility was more or less just to touch base with Him about other people.

I certainly didn't understand that interceding for someone could change them and *me*. I had always wrestled with how much difference my involvement actually made when I prayed for other people. What good was interceding if I didn't know what to pray for? What words would I even say? Since God knew what people needed, and I didn't, I couldn't really imagine that my involvement was particularly helpful. Wasn't God sovereign? Would He accomplish His will for other people without my prayers?

Here's what I learned during our college ministry years:[40] 1) Intercessory prayer is about seeing the world through God's eyes and praying about what He deems important. 2) Intercession is my response to His mission. Prayer is no mantra, no rabbit's foot, no brownie-point system. It's essential to my own perspective and spiritual walk.

My understanding of what God's up to is inconsequential.

JOINING HIM IN HIS WORK

Instead of praying for God to reveal His will and waiting around for a lightning bolt to strike in the correct location, we ought to busy ourselves doing whatever ministry is right under our noses. This means engaging hurting people, praying for unresolved situations, and volunteering wherever we see ministry needs, regardless of how those needs match our spiritual gifting. We should reconsider how we use the phrase "if it's your will" when we pray.

"If it's your will" can easily become the cliché we add to our requests and intercessions when we're not convinced what God wants to do in a situation. We must resist accepting the erroneous belief that prayer is about getting God to do something we think He should do.

Powerful prayers require us to hear God's voice and join Him in His work. If you begin praying for God's mind instead of God's will, you will have His mind; then you will naturally understand His will and desire to do it. Plus, there will be a lot less waiting around for lightning strikes.

Now for the next logical question: How are you supposed to know where God's working? When it comes to understanding where you should invest your time, you probably feel pulled in a dozen directions. Everything in your life seems critically and equally important. The voices from each priority clamor for your attention. *You should lead a small group. You should get a new job. You should spend more time with your kids. You should lose weight. You should work in children's church.* No wonder we don't know what to pray for. We don't even know what voice to listen to.

Successful prayer, especially intercessory prayer, has essentially one key ingredient: hearing from God. Praying for something that God isn't ready to do is like trying to swipe yourself into a hotel room and realizing you're at the wrong door. (I've done that many times—very frustrating, not to mention embarrassing). Your intentions are good, but the door isn't going to open for you. Instead of feeling frustrated with God for not answering, we just need to move down the hallway to the correct door. Choosing the right door, (i.e. hearing God's voice) means you are able to respond to the Holy Spirit's prompting, not that God has given you the blueprint for the next big event in someone's life.

God called Moses to ministry at the burning bush by confronting him with a crisis decision point—accept and engage in the supernatural, or pass by and resume his easier, less impactful life. Moses took the first option. He responded by entering God's presence and worshipping.

I want the kind of power and influence that Moses had, not because I hope to part seas or turn walking sticks into serpents, but because I want God's power on the people I love and the ministry where I've invested my life. I can no longer pass up the supernatural and find satisfaction in the mundane. I want more from Him and for Him.

MAKING AGREEMENT

The definition of *intercede* is "to plead or make a request on behalf of another; to intervene for the purpose of producing agreement; mediate."[41] When Jesus intercedes for us to the Father, He mediates agreement between the two parties. He interprets our frailties and explains our motives to God Almighty, Who can't look on sin. As the intercessor, Jesus' heart is pure, with love for both parties. He seeks agreement for both. Jesus hears the Father's voice, knows the Father's heart, and responds accordingly on our behalf.

Intercession is the most selfless kind of prayer. It approaches God's throne on behalf of someone else, someone whose choices don't affect you and who might not even change. It's not a run-of-the-mill request. When you intercede for someone else, you act as a translator: your prayers seek to reinterpret your requests to the will of God the Father. You allow the Holy Spirit to cause agreement between the two.

Herein lies one of the difficulties in knowing God's will and acting on it—we often aren't sure what God wants or even what to pray for. We hesitate to involve ourselves in people's problems because we don't want to jump out unnecessarily on their behalf.

We need to grow in our confidence of recognizing God's voice and trusting it. Whenever I have an authoritative or creative thought, I consider that the communication is coming from God, and I analyze it. John instructs his readers in this process in 1 Jn. 4:1—"Dear friends, do not believe every spirit, but test the spirits to see whether they are from God." The Greek word for "do not believe" is *pisteuō* ("to believe, be persuaded of"); the word for "test" is *dokimazō* ("to examine, prove, or scrutinize").[42] Don't trust your gut—compare your thoughts with Scriptural truth! If it matches the Bible, assume that the message is from the Holy Spirit.

RECOGNIZING THE VOICE

If your heart is pure and open to God's voice, your next concern will be knowing who to pray for. In my early days of interceding, I noticed that people didn't just walk up to me and tell me their hidden issues—no college students admitted being anorexic or alcoholic or sexually active. They just smiled and came to Bible study. No church people said their marriages were failing or their kids were addicts or they were drowning in debt. They just smiled and came to church.

Intercession requires discernment. How would I know when God was calling me to pray or help someone? Enter the Holy Spirit and some good advice from a friend, who told me that any time a person's face popped into my head, I should consider it a prompting from the Holy Spirit and pray for that person. If I thought of some way to help that person, I should do it. That was God speaking to me about a need.

I decided to field-test the theory.

The next time someone's face flew through my brain, I sent a note to that person and said that I was praying for her, encouraging her to keep trusting God. I found out later that she had just caught her teenage daughter in a sexual relationship, and her despair had consumed her; the encouragement came at the perfect time.

I took a bag of groceries to a young mother from church; when she opened her front door, she started crying. Her husband's business was tanking, and they had no money for food. They hadn't told anyone.

I appeared at the door of a neighborhood mom to whom I hadn't spoken for over a year because I became suddenly worried about her. That day she was packing her house to move, and she felt overwhelmed with sadness. We prayed together.

It turns out that I'm surrounded by people in pain. I had never recognized the Holy Spirit's voice until I made a point to listen for it.

With new faith and new resolve, my husband and I began praying for anyone and everyone we thought of. We woke in the middle of the night with people on our minds and in our dreams. It seemed that God was sending us a never-ending flood of folks who needed spiritual covering. It was exhilarating, weighty, and exhausting. Could God really be calling us to lose sleep over other people?

> "Could God really be calling us to lose sleep over other people?"

Are other people really my problem? Yes, they are. Does spending time, energy, and even sleep for someone else clash with our mode of living? Yes, it does.

You probably grew up hearing your mom recite the Golden Rule whenever you refused to play with your sibling: "Do unto others as you would have them do unto you." Maybe you were the quick-witted kid who retorted, "I just want to be left alone." In other words, *She's not my problem.*

Go away. Then everyone's happy.

The fatal flaw with this mentality, according to Jesus, is that He created us to live in community, the one shining hallmark of the church. It's not our fancy buildings and cafés, not our famous worship leaders, not our best-selling Christian books. Not even our holy living, because we all know we're not that holy. Jesus said, "By *this* everyone will know that you are my disciples, *if you love one another.*"[43] Love and intercession are sacrificial gifts from you to someone else Jesus loves.

We are the exact opposite of the church Jesus created when we don't carry each other's burdens. Paul called this the "law

of Christ" in Galatians 6:2. A law is a basic, bare-bones require-
ment. A minimal expectation for the good of a community.

TAPESTRY

The church provides the context through which we can remain aware of others' needs. The relationships we forge and
maintain provide the fabric of the Christian church. Up close,
church is a myriad of threads—conversations, activities, worshipping, laboring, disagreeing—but together the threads
weave a beautiful tapestry of God's love. According to Paul, in
his letter to the Ephesians, intercessory prayer is an important
thread of Christian culture: "With all prayer and petition pray
at all times in the Spirit, and with this in view, be on the alert
with all perseverance and petition for all the saints."[44] In other
words, be discerning and pray for each other because trouble
will most certainly head your way at some point.

We don't necessarily know if our prayers will make any
difference in another person's life; we might not even stay in
the relationship long enough to find out. That's where faith
takes over, and incidentally, where growth occurs. We may
never find out what happens to someone we have prayed for,
but we'll have an eternity to find out. The results of intercession are God's business; we have merely been called to pray.
Charles Spurgeon said, "If sinners be damned, at least let them
leap to Hell over our bodies. If they will perish, let them perish with our arms about their knees. Let no one go there un-
warned and un-prayed for."[45]

Intercession packs an emotional punch. It's a whopper
of a prayer, meant for the serious prayer-makers among us
who recognize that other people *are* our problem. We *are* our
brother's keepers. It's how the world will recognize Christ in
us and stir in them a hunger for relationship with Him. "By
this all men will know that you are my disciples, if you love
one another."[46]

Do you want to stop feeling jealous, critical, vengeful, or hurt? Intercede for those people you feel negatively towards. Jesus says in Matt. 5:44, "But I say to you, love your enemies and pray for those who persecute you, that you may be sons of your Father in heaven." *You!* Your prayer is not intended to change your persecutors—it's intended to change *you!*

PRAYER OF INTERCESSION

You can make a difference by interceding. Try these two prayers of intercession.

Jesus' prayer in John 17:20-23:
I pray also for those who will believe in me through their message, that all of them may be one, Father, just as you are in me and I am in you. May they also be in us so that the world may believe that you have sent me. I have given them the glory that you gave me, that they may be one as we are one; I in them and you in me. May they be brought to complete unity to let the world know that you send me and have loved them even as you have loved me.

My prayer from John 17:
Dear Lord in Heaven, I pray for Your love and protection over _____. Help _____ to see your glory in the world, wherever _____ might go, that Your presence will be there, reminding him/her of Your unfailing love. I ask the Holy Spirit to move in _____ and bring him/her into a knowledge and understanding of Your love and sacrifice. Please save _____ and make him/her your child in Your perfect timing. Use me as an instrument of encouragement and compassion. Help me not to push ahead of the work You are already doing in his/her life. Amen.

CHAPTER 14
IN THE QUIET PLACES

SEVERAL YEARS AGO, when our oldest son entered high school, I started a little prayer group specifically to pray over our children and their public schools. God brought five women together. None of us were close friends previously, but we all had the same desire, as well as an assortment of elementary, middle school, and high school students. Two had one child in college. With the exception of me, everyone had a combination of boys and girls, but mostly boys.

On the first Friday of every month, we labored before the Lord together over the hearts and minds of our children. We prayed for their friends, their dating relationships, their future spouses, their goals and dreams. We prayed against the influence of culture, media, wrong friends, sexual sin, and dangerous role models. We shared with each other our children's triumphs—sports, music, and education—with mutual joy and celebration; we collaborated over parenting, punishment, and spiritual development. Linking souls, we cried in one voice to the Lord of heaven.

We watched miracles unfold in our families. Shy and awkward children found confidence and talent. Lonely children found friends. Our children joined FCA, Young Life, and Campus Crusade. They went on mission trips and counseled at camps and received calls to ministry. They have gone into art, medicine, engineering, politics, counseling, teaching, entrepreneurship, and ministry. They are getting married to Christians and having children and serving in their churches.

But make no mistake. The enemy wages war against families who pray with clean hands and pure hearts. We are still praying for our kids—now young adults—against the grip and pressure of success, materialism, ambition, sexual sin, addiction, and unbelief. And the reason we fight these battles in prayer is because we have seen the power of God on our children, and we know they can't survive without it. It's why we pray and why we believe that God will answer us. He has to answer. He has promised, "For where two or three gather in my name, there am I with them."[47]

Many people in the Bible made requests together. Collectively, their prayer lives changed the course of history. Daniel, Shadrach, Meshach, and Abednego prayed all night until Daniel received the king's dream and its interpretation, which saved their lives and the lives of all the counselors in Babylon. Their prayers even thwarted executions via hungry lions and a fiery furnace. After Daniel was lifted from the lions' den, the Medo-Persian King Darius declared Jehovah to be the one, true God.[48]

Esther and her maidens, with the prayers of Mordecai and the Jewish people, fasted and prayed for three days before she entered the king's presence unannounced to plead for reversal of a planned genocide. She saved an entire race of people.[49]

After Jesus ascended into heaven, the disciples gathered all of Jesus' followers in an upper room to pray. Their lives were in jeopardy, yet their mission lay ahead of them. The Holy Spirit descended on their heads like fire, infusing them with miraculous powers to heal disease, raise the dead, preach in foreign languages, and withstand persecution. They started a movement called "The Way," which was later termed "Christianity."[50] These simple men and women changed history forever by establishing the concept of the church: a place to fellowship, serve, grow, and worship together.

Find a group with clean hands and pure hearts. Trust them with your requests. Then storm the gates of heaven and hell together.

BEGINNING TO INTERCEDE

How, exactly, does intercession work? What should regular people do, if in fact, regular people can intercede for others? How can you make a difference by praying for someone else?

Let's start by looking at some examples of intercessors in the Bible.

Paul was confident that he would be delivered from his imprisonment because the Philippians were praying for him (Phil. 1:19)

- James believed intercessory prayers could heal the sick (Jms. 5:14-15)
- Moses believed God would heal his sister Miriam from the leprosy that had been a punishment for her sin (Num. 12:3)
- The Israelites' welfare in captivity correlated to their prayers for their captors (Jer. 29:7)
- Jesus prayed for Peter's faith to return after he betrayed Jesus, and for Peter's influence on the church (Lk. 22:32-33)
- The Corinthians prayed for Paul's success in ministry; he attributes blessings to their prayers (2 Cor. 1:11)
- Paul prayed for Jews' salvation (Rom. 10:1)
- Jesus prayed for the forgiveness of his enemies as He hung on the cross (Lk. 23:34)

THE HEART OF INTERCESSING

A curious thought hit me while I read these stories of intercession. I would have expected the intercessors and the people they prayed for to be in sync with each other, understanding the same needs and making the same prayer requests. You know, Miriam calls Moses and says,

"Moses, could you come pray for me because I have leprosy now, and God listens to you the best? And by the way, I'm sorry I gossiped about your wife. Aaron and I have been a little jealous of all the attention you get. Let's pray together so God will heal me."

No. That's not how it happened. God struck Miriam with leprosy for her sinful attitude and actions, and Moses fell on his knees for her. There's no mention of Miriam's repentance. With the exception of Paul's churches praying for him, these other intercessors were praying for people *who hadn't yet repented.* In fact, throughout Scripture, most of the time, prophets, priests, and apostles pray for people *who aren't concerned about their spiritual state.*

In other words, the faith necessary for powerful intercession lies in the intercessor's heart, not the heart of the person prayed for. Perhaps intercessory prayer is more about the intercessors' *soulspeak* to God than it is about accomplishing anything tangible (although that often happens, too).

Moses consistently intercedes for the Israelites (for their provision, safety, and lives), even while they grumble about everything God provides for them. Moses, not the Israelites, has faith in God. Moses' intercession for Israel creates something tangible (manna, water, quail, protection from Egypt, among other things). Whenever God meets the Israelites' physical needs, they begin remembering His love for them.

Although Moses' intercession propels the Israelites forward on their spiritual journey, over the course of 40 years in the wilderness, their spiritual state barely changes at all. You could argue that it worsened, since the adults who left Egypt weren't allowed to enter the Promised Land.

I believe that Moses' intercession was a natural response to his relationship with God, not a Christian leadership strategy. "The Lord would speak to Moses face to face, as a man speaks with his friend."[51] Friend to friend. Not friend for friend. God and Moses interacted because of their intimacy.

THAT HOLY SPIRIT POWER

The Holy Spirit superintends all intercessory prayer. For some reason, God desires for us to participate in the stories of others. The proof of the Holy Spirit's promptings in our hearts is revealed in the way we treat others.[52] Our desire to make intercessory prayers directly correlates to our acknowledgement and reception of the Holy Spirit's work in our lives. Paul concludes his teaching about the fruits of Spirit-living like this: "Since we are living by the Spirit, let us follow the Spirit's leading in every part of our lives."[53]

If you want to intercede, you must be willing to hear from the Holy Spirit. Experience doesn't matter. Using novices is just the kind of thing God likes to do.

HOW TO INTERCEDE

How can you become an intercessor? By now, you know what I'm going to suggest: you must speak from the soul. It might involve some agony. Even if you're an Academy Award winner, you can't fake agony, especially not in front of God, so don't try. Start with worship and pray your way towards soul transformation. Intercession will ensue.

HEARING GOD

The book of 1 Samuel follows the life of a prophet whose powerful ministry spanned the end of the judges' rule through the first king of Israel. The man Samuel knew how to pray effectively, and his prayers began with his remarkable ability to hear God's voice. Not surprisingly, Samuel's life began with a prayer, an earnest request from his mother Hannah, who promised to give her first child back to the Lord in service for his whole life, if only she could conceive.

Samuel's story is riveting. One night, God calls to Samuel while he's lying in bed. He is a little boy who works for Eli, the High Priest of Israel. Three times, Samuel hears his name called, and each time he assumes the voice is Eli's, so he asks Eli what he needs him to do. After Samuel wakes Eli the third time, the priest realizes what's happening. Eli tells Samuel, "The Lord is calling you. Next time, say, 'Speak, Lord, for your servant is listening.'"

Samuel waits. "The Lord came and stood there, calling as at other times, 'Samuel! Samuel!'"[54] *God stood there!* (Let that sink in a minute.) Samuel waits quietly and expectantly, and God comes to speak to him. Samuel learns that he must sit and wait for God if he wants to hear His will.[55]

MAKING TIME FOR THE QUIET

Throughout Scripture, God speaks to open hearts when they listen for Him. God instructs Moses in the stillness; He inspires David in the pasture; He calms Elijah after the storm passes; He comforts Jesus in the Garden. God never feels hurried, so He will not coerce you or rush you or hunt you down in your busyness and drag you off to the wilderness. He will wait and speak when you are ready to listen.

A busy, demanding lifestyle may be the greatest spiritual weapon ever invented for assaulting the warriors of Christ. Busyness distracts our focus, enslaves our desires, diverts our calling, and undermines our values. It keeps us from hearing God when we need to.

In the beginning, God specifically designed a garden setting for His interaction with mankind. He knew that men and women needed a quiet space to maintain relationship with Him. When Adam and Eve disobey God, they break the easy fellowship they enjoy, and God must eject them from the Garden of Eden. Mankind then entered a world forever dominated by chaos, noise, selfishness, and weariness. The struggle to know God had begun.

DISCERNING GOD'S WILL

Job was another man who heard God's voice. You may remember his hardships from our discussion on lamentation. Job poured out his heart to God: he raged, he cried, he asked, without response. Then, while he sat and waited, he pondered and considered his heart. I suspect that after a few weeks of unanswered misery, Job began to question the assumptions he had about God. He began to wait with purpose. He listened for God to speak.

WISDOM THROUGH OBEDIENCE

Proverbs 3:5-6 implores us to "Trust in the Lord in all your heart and lean not on your own understanding; in all your ways acknowledge him, and he will make your path straight." The straight path mentioned here is a pathway of correction and growth, not a scenic meandering lane. When you trust God's words, God will straighten your paths, which by nature will be crooked from wandering aimlessly, looking for direction and fulfillment in life. Under the harshest trials, you will sometimes confuse truth with pragmatism and veer off the course God has designed for you. What you need is spiritual discernment, not a practical plan, and discernment is the spiritual reward of choosing to trust and glorify God. The painful process of having God realign your path cultivates discernment in your spirit.

Spiritual discernment saved Job from agreeing with his well-intentioned friends who begged him to confess his sin so God would start blessing him again (*bad things happen to bad people and good things happen to good people*). Instead, Job surrendered to accepting his circumstances, without knowing a plausible reason:

> "I know that you can do all things; no plan of yours can be thwarted. You asked, 'Who is this that obscures my counsel without knowledge?' Surely I spoke of things I did not understand, things too wonderful for me to know . . . . My ears had heard of you but now my eyes have seen you.[56]

> After the Lord had said these things to Job, he said to Eliphaz the Temanite, 'I am angry with you and your two friends, because you have not spoken of me what is right, as my servant Job has. So now take seven bulls and seven rams and go to my servant Job and sacrifice a burnt offering for yourselves. My servant Job will pray for you, and I will accept his prayer and not deal with you according to your folly. You have not spoken of me what is right, as my servant Job has.'"[57]

Job summed up the ordeal like this: "Now my eyes have seen you." Perhaps that was God's goal all along?

INTERCEDING FOR OTHERS

Our last intercessor, Abraham, can be found sitting at the door of his tent during the hottest part of the day, as three men appear a distance away. Turns out, two of the men are angels, and one is the Lord. He has come to speak to Abraham and inform him of two plans: 1) Sarah will conceive and birth that long-awaited baby, even though she's 90 years old; and 2) God will destroy Sodom and Gomorrah for their sexual perversion (Abraham's nephew Lot lives there). So the two angels leave to demolish Sodom and escort Lot and his family from the city before it burns with fire and brimstone.

CONVERSING, FRIEND TO FRIEND

The Lord stays to talk with Abraham, because that's what God does with people who hear and discern His voice. Abraham has secured a special place as "the friend of God."[58] So after Abraham hears the impending doom of Lot's family, he intercedes for them—he mediates—with the God of the universe, for his frustrating, screw-up of a nephew.

"The faith necessary for powerful intercession lies in the intercessors' heart, not the heart of the person prayed for."

Abraham likely remembers the day he gave Lot first choice of the land, and Lot chose Sodom, a city without any righteous people. Maybe Abraham relives his memories of assembling an army from his own 318 men and racing after four kings to rescue Lot from them. I imagine Abraham can recall in an instant every flaw in Lot's character over the decades of their relationship—Lot's irresponsibility, argumentativeness, greed. Lot has sown his own trouble, and he is reaping the harvest. Yet his loving uncle feels compelled to get involved, again.

PLEADING, SERVANT TO LORD

Abraham implores God to change His mind about destroying Lot and his city. Starting with "what if there are 50 righteous people?" and ending with "What if there are ten?" Abraham negotiates an escape for Lot. Six times, he broaches a new deal with God so Lot can be spared.

But Lot is his own worst enemy. In the end, Lot still loses his prestige, his wealth, his wife, his home, two future sons-in-law, and his self-respect. Alone in the wilderness, his two virgin daughters get him drunk and have sex with him so they can bear children. Except for Peter's explanation of Lot's "righteous soul," we wouldn't know if Lot believed in the Lord or not.[59]

Abraham changed God's mind, and God changed Abraham's faith. But Lot didn't seem to change at all.[60]

SOLITUDE

How did Abraham recognize that his visitor was God Himself? And how did he feel comfortable enough to bargain for Lot's life? Where did Job find the courage to trust God through his suffering and loss? How did Moses, Elijah, Daniel, Esther, or Paul hear God's voice and discern God's will for their lives during their greatest trials?

They met God in the lonely places, in solitude of emptiness. They enclosed themselves in rooms with friends and fasted. They retreated to the wilderness and waited. They climbed mountains and expected God to pass by.

We can't deny the correlation between Jesus' lifestyle of prayer and solitude because powerful miracles followed His moments of isolation. Whenever Jesus "retreated to a solitary place and prayed" He returned to His ministry and healed disease, cast out demons, and raised the dead. He always returned to His ministry with extraordinary power.[61]

TOPICS OF INTERCESSORY PRAYER

Okay, sign me up! I'm ready to intercede, you say. What will you pray about? Consider these topics of intercession in the Bible:

- for your enemies—Mtt. 5:43-48, Lk. 6:27-31
- to empower others to ministry and spiritual growth—2 Thess. 1:10-12, Col. 1:9-14
- the spread of the gospel—Col. 4:3
- preservation from harm and courage to withstand danger—Esther 4:15-16
- protection from the Devil and the world—Jn. 17:9-26
- repentance and forgiveness for sin—Job 42:7-10

WHAT GOD SOUNDS LIKE

An important discussion involves discerning God's voice from my own voice or from the Devil's (remember, he is an angel of light).[62] You may never have thought about it before, but when you hear God speak to you, the voice will generally sound like you, only much wiser. Whenever you have solutions, ideas, and advice that have far more discernment and godliness behind them than you can attribute to your intelligence, that's probably God talking. Sometimes, another person will give you a piece of advice or a perspective, and your heart will quicken inside your chest, or you will speak truth and wisdom more articulate and eloquent than you've ever spoken before. You might be filled with inspiration, an idea, or a thought too wonderful to be yours. You suddenly have insight into a complex situation or take command against the forces of evil. These are all examples of hearing and responding to God's voice.

God can speak through anybody, but an intercessor must groom the ability to hear God speak at any and every opportunity. (Remember Abraham? You never know when three guys will show up at your door with bad news and you might be called on to save someone's life.)

In her book *Becoming a Prayer Warrior*, Elizabeth Alves gives a simple but profound explanation for discerning God's voice from the temptations of the enemy: "God leads; Satan drives. God convicts; Satan condemns. God woos; Satan tugs hard."[63] Remember, God isn't in a hurry. He leads us along gently, even amidst the hard times. He doesn't push you or coerce you into following His will. If you are listening to Him, you will hear His wisdom for what's happening around you.

REVIEW OF INTERCESSION:

Take a look at the main points from this chapter on intercession. As you begin to intercede for others, you should incorporate these truths into your life.

- Intercession brings others' needs before God's throne
- You must create moments of silence and waiting if you want to hear God speak
- God reveals His will through obedient response and expectant waiting
- Discernment grows from faith, when your suffering would suggest other responses
- Intercession changes you; you can't pray for other people and not love them

PRAYER OF INTERCESSION

Let's read two of Jesus' intercessory prayers and learn how to formulate a prayer that isn't about us. (That's harder than it sounds.)

Jesus' prayer in John 17:9-11, 15-17:
I pray for them. I am not praying for the world but for those you have given me, for they are yours. All I have is yours, and all you have is mine. And glory has come to me through them. I will remain in the world no longer, but they are still in the world, and I am coming to you. Holy Father, protect them by the power of your name—the name you gave me—so that they may be one as we are one. . . . My prayer is not that you take them out of the world but that you protect them from the evil one. . . . Sanctify them by the truth; your word is truth.

My prayer from John 17:
God, I stand in awe of your great power. Everything I have is from you, and I thank you for the many blessings in my life, even the situations and people who frustrate and anger me. I ask you to protect _____ by the power of your great name. Give me the strength and love to reflect your love to _____ so that we can be unified in the body of Christ. I pray for the lost world to see Jesus through my actions and faith. In Jesus' name, Amen.

PART 8: "BACK OFF, BUSTER!"—SPEAKING SPIRITUAL WARFARE

The Lord is my light and my salvation—
Whom shall I fear?
The Lord is the stronghold of my life—
Of whom shall I be afraid?
When evil men advance against me to devour my flesh,
When my enemies and my foes attack me,
They will stumble and fall.
Though an army besiege me,
My heart will not fear;
Though war break out against me,
even then will I be confident.
One thing I ask of the Lord,
this is what I seek:
that I may dwell in the house of the Lord
all the days of my life,
to gaze upon the beauty of the Lord
and to seek him in his temple.
For in the day of trouble he will keep me safe in his dwelling;

He will hide me in the shelter of his tabernacle
And set me high upon a rock.
Hear my voice when I call, O Lord;
Be merciful to me and answer me.
My heart says of you, "Seek his face!"
Your face, Lord, I will seek.
Psalm 27

CHAPTER 15
NOT A SUPERHERO

IT WAS SHORTLY after 2:30 in the afternoon. The gray highway rippled under late-August heat as Shane and I headed for the ocean, our back seat filled with college students, chatting energetically. We had left our children for the weekend under the care of our trusted babysitter Anna. Now a young adult, Anna had babysat our boys since she was a teenager in our youth group.

We weren't in the car long when fear gripped me. "I have a sick feeling in my stomach all of a sudden," I said. "I'm worried about the kids."

I am really not a paranoid mother, no matter what my kids say about me. Early in our parenting, Shane and I had established the habit of leaving our boys with babysitters so Shane and I could enjoy weekly dates, serve at retreats and camps, and attend conferences. During Shane's business years, we routinely took company trips out of the country and left the kids with our parents. While I often felt panic on the first day of a long trip abroad, I found I could handle the separation well if I prayed often and called home some.

That day in the car, while we drove toward our beach retreat, I walked myself through my post-leaving pep-talk routine: *This is only the first day. I've only been gone two hours. The kids will be fine. The panic will pass.*

But it didn't.

This weekend marked an important college retreat for our ministry at VCU. We were traveling to a large beach home in the Outer Banks, owned by a student's parents, for a student leadership retreat. I had spent the last few days meal-planning and shopping for the event, while Shane had organized the schedule and prepared the seminars.

The retreat was occurring at the perfect time for our college ministry. We were experiencing positive momentum; students were grasping God's love and feeling a mission to reach their campus for Jesus. Our weekly Bible study felt poised to explode. We believed that God would unleash His Spirit at this retreat, and we had readied ourselves to see God empower students to overcome sin patterns and bond together as a team. We were praying for energy to represent Christ on a campus that writhed under palatable satanic oppression and influence.

And here I was, overwhelmed and anxious about leaving my children for three days. Was this merely a distraction?

"Just pray," Shane said.

"I have been. I can't shake the nausea in my stomach. I keep thinking that someone's in danger. I'm worried about Brady. Anna is taking the kids to the pool this afternoon." Our youngest, Brady, had begun swimming around the pool unassisted, with his swim vest on. He had just turned three years old.

Shane joined me in prayer, and we asked the Lord for His protection over our children and wisdom for Anna. We prayed against the Devil, who desired harm to our children and disunity to our college ministry. We prayed in the Spirit. My stomach kept churning.

We asked the college students to pray with us. We prayed again out loud. The car fell into awkward silence while we drove along. I was still worried, but the nausea passed.

About 30 minutes later, I received a call on my cell phone.

"Hello?" I said uncertainly. (It was before the days of caller I.D. on cell phones.)

It was Anna.

"Everything's okay, but I need to tell you what happened." I could hear her voice shaking. "We went to the pool. During adult swim, I took Brady's vest off and got the kids a snack. When I turned around, I couldn't see Brady anywhere. I ran up and down the side of the pool looking for him in the water. Then I saw him, lying on the bottom of the pool, flapping his arms. He was trying to swim. He looked up at me, and our eyes met—I will never forget that look!" Anna was crying, struggling to continue. "I screamed, but no one moved. The lifeguards didn't even see what was happening. Nobody noticed him at all."

"What happened?" My heart was hammering.

"I dove in and pulled him up to the surface. He's okay now. He's just really scared. We all are!"

I was crying with her, thinking of Brady and remembering the car ride. "What time did this happen?"

"About 2:50, when the adult swim time started."

While we prayed.

The forces of hell had prepared an assault on our family and our ministry, and the forces of heaven took up weapons and met them head-on.

SECRET WEAPON

If you're following God, and even if you're not, you probably want to pray like that. You want your prayers to *change things*, even things you're not aware of. You want to pray into the unexpected places like swimming pools and automobiles and canyon trails. You want your soul's words to alter the trajectory of someone's life.

Maybe you buy one of the 100,000 books on prayer and read up on why you should pray and how to pray. You try keeping prayer journals and prayer calendars. You go on prayer walks.

These are all good ideas, but honestly, when you pray, it doesn't matter *what* you do. It matters *why* you do it. You must speak from your soul and listen with your soul.

Spiritual warfare is the secret weapon in the arsenal of prayer. If you understand this kind of prayer—if you actually pray this kind of prayer—it will change everything. Your life will transform. Being Christlike means seeing like Christ saw, living like Christ lived, praying like Christ prayed, and fighting like Christ fought.

Oh, yes. Jesus fights. Yes, He loves everyone, He turns the other cheek, He's the Prince of Peace—but make no mistake. Jesus is a fierce warrior. He vanquished His enemy all the way to death and beyond.

Jesus is peaceful toward *us*, the object of His affection and sacrifice, but He is not peaceful toward His enemy. He has eyes like fire, and He carries a sword. Jesus understands His battle, His enemy, His allies, and most importantly—the ramifications of losing. And Jesus doesn't lose. That is not possible. And that's the power we summon when we pray.

UNCOMFORTABLE

Spiritual warfare might make you uncomfortable. It should. I guess we are generally content to live our lives in blissful ignorance of the war that rages around us. We consider spiritual warfare on the Sundays that our pastors preach from Ephesians 6 or 1 Peter 5:8. You get it already. Satan is a roaring lion, and he's out to get you.

That's a little unnerving, so by 4 p.m. on a Sunday, you've put it out of your mind. Thinking the Devil is around every corner, waiting to devour you is a hard way to live. You believe in his contextual existence, of course; he is the proverbial bad-guy who works through drugs and mass media and pornography. None of these are problems for you, so you're good.

Because you're uncomfortable thinking about spiritual war, you prefer to fight your Christian battles on a more manageable level. You employ the time-proven control method called *worry.* You worry about money and relationships and needs. But you don't really worry about *influence.*

My real fear—if I'll admit it—is that I feel as if God can't beat the Devil. You know, the Devil does seem to win a lot of battles. (Just watch the news.) Sometimes it seems as if God has run out of strength to intervene in the affairs of mankind. Maybe God can't remember anymore how to raise the dead or give sight to the blind. I've never seen it happen, so maybe God's not so powerful after all.

No, you say. That can't be true! If it were true, then everything I believe would be false, so it must be true.

And if it is true—if God can still do all those things—then the problem must lie with us. Whenever God's power sits un-

> "Jesus doesn't lose. That is not possible. And that's the power we summon when we pray."

challenged, untapped, and unleashed, our faithlessness is interfering with His work. He is a miracle-worker. That is God's character. The subsequent conclusion must be this: our lives hold greater possibility for monumental impact than we realize or believe.

According to Jesus, you are supposed to be a part of His miracle business. You have supernatural powers at your disposal, even if you're afraid to put on the cape.

You? A superhero? I know what you're feeling. *I can't. I'm afraid.*

Why? Because if we acknowledge that God can manifest Himself however He chooses, we must release control so He can do it. A life released to God's will becomes a life under God's total control, about Him and His agenda only.

But God will never force Himself on us; if we lack miraculous intervention of God in our lives, it's because we haven't welcomed it. We are either afraid of it, or we don't believe it exists.

This takes us back to the beginning of the book. Are you willing to worship God for who He is, even the parts you don't understand, the parts that scare you? If you desire comprehending the complexities of a supernatural God, you must choose faith. You will never figure Him out; you can't control Him or contain Him. You can only decide to invite Him or decide not to invite Him. Go ahead—invite the Holy Spirit! Just prepare yourself to watch His mighty power transform your life.

JUST A REGULAR PERSON

You say you're just a regular person. You don't do weird stuff. I'm a regular person, too; however, I would like an extraordinary prayer life. I've witnessed enough little glimpses of powerful prayer to see that it actually works. And I want more of it.

Don't worry; I'm not about to launch into a tutorial about praying in the Spirit or finding your prayer language or waving incense at people. That's between you and God. But I believe that you can welcome the power of the Holy Spirit into your prayer life. You just have to ask Him for it. God works in and through us in creative fashion. We just need to let Him be God.

Why am I confident that He will give you power? Consider again Jesus' explanation of a father who meets his children's needs:

> "So I say to you: Ask and it will be given to you; seek and you will find; knock and the door will be opened to you. For everyone who asks receives; the one who seeks finds; and to the one who knocks, the door will be opened. Which of you fathers, if your son asks for a fish, will give him a snake instead? Or if he asks for an egg, will give

him a scorpion? If you then, though you are evil, know how to give good gifts to your children, how much more will your Father in heaven *give the Holy Spirit to those who ask him!*"[64]

The Holy Spirit's powerful acts validate Jesus' deity. Miracles point people to the authenticity of Jesus' ministry and His sacrifice on the cross today, just as they did in Jesus' time.

Does your faith grow when you read about God's power in the Bible? Since God never changes, let's assume that God still has the same power now that He had in the Bible. He can accomplish anything He wants. He can stop time or help you walk on water. He can cure disease.

Just because you don't see God waging these wars doesn't mean the wars aren't happening. If you lived in Asia or Africa, you might see God's mighty acts of power every day. In places like these, darkness is so oppressive that prayer warriors approach the throne of God with a boldness that would shock most of us in the West. Prayer warriors there see leprosy cured, blindness healed, the dead raised to life, and demons exorcized. Apparently, God hasn't forgotten how to do anything.

Here in Western cultured society, we're too controlling and self-aware to welcome the clash of the Holy Spirit against fate. We've got science and medicine and technology to lean on. We have services to run and programs to monitor. We have schedules. The Holy Spirit just needs to show up at the allotted times. You know, during the invitation. We've got the rest covered.

PRAYING SPIRITUAL WARFARE

This is a good prayer to read up on—who waged spiritual warfare in the Bible and how did they do it? It might keep you from being persuaded to pray how other people say you should pray. Notice what Jesus does. Then pray your own, maybe something like mine.

Jesus' prayer in John 17:15-17, 18:36, 3:3:
My prayer is not that you take them out of the world but that you protect them from the evil one. They are not of the world, even as I am not of it. Sanctify them by the truth; your word is truth . . . My kingdom is not of this world . . . I tell you the truth, no one can see the kingdom of God unless he is born again.

My Prayer from John 17:
Dear Lord in heaven, may we focus on your mission to reach the world. I ask that You help us to hear the truth and recognize it. I pray in Jesus' name for You to bind the deceiver of our souls, to block his lies and open our hearts and minds to believe and receive your truth. You have left us here in this world, so equip us for powerful ministry. I pray that we will build Your kingdom, and not our own. Bind the king of this world and the demons that serve him. Make us vigilant in our fight. Protect and empower us, in Jesus' name, Amen.

CHAPTER 16
GREATER THINGS

AFTER SEVEN YEARS of campus ministry, Shane took a pastoral position at a church in our city. A couple years into this position, Shane got a call from a desperate man named Frank, asking to get together. He was a homeless middle-aged man who had been rotating between shelters and park benches for the better part of four years.

Apparently, he had frequented one of our free campus outdoor breakfasts three years prior and picked up Shane's business card somewhere between the free pancakes and the plastic silverware. Frank had kept Shane's card in his wallet ever since. Maybe it was his get-out-of-jail-free card—his last connection to God, if he ever needed it.

This time, he needed help, and he wasn't too ashamed to ask for it. Shane agreed to meet Frank downtown for coffee. Given Frank's wanton condition, coffee turned into a big dinner. I was home with the kids, praying for Shane's wisdom, protection, and discernment while I went about my evening routine.

While Frank used the restroom at the restaurant, Shane called to give me a quick update. He thought Frank was oppressed by demons. I said something like, "Cut the dinner short and get home now." (I'm spiritual like that.)

After an hour had passed without Shane showing up, I began picturing a dark alley with Frank standing over my husband's dead body chopped into a hundred tiny pieces. I started thinking about how I would tell the kids that their father died at the hands of a madman.

Then Shane called again. "Honey, is it okay if I bring Frank home to spend the night? He's catching a bus to Portland in the morning."

"What? Isn't he demon-possessed?"

"Well, I'm not sure if it was oppression or possession, but it was something. He had the crazy eyes and the weird voice going on. It was scary for a while there. But I prayed over him and commanded the demons to leave in Jesus' name. He's good now."

"You did what?!" Shane is authoritative and all, but *demons*?

"Is it okay if I bring him home?"

My voice sounded like an old reel-to-reel movie when the tape catches in the projector, slow and underwater. "You—want—to—bring—him—home?"

"It's the best option for Frank. He wanted money for a ticket to Portland, where he can stay with his brother and look for a job. I didn't want to just give him that much cash, so I took him to the bus station and bought the ticket for him. He planned on sleeping in the station until his bus leaves tomorrow, but I don't think that's a good idea. You know the verse about one demon leaving and seven more coming?"[65]

Yes, I did know. Hence, the reason for my question.

Frank came home. I made up the hide-a-bed in the basement (not a great bed, but I was afraid to put him upstairs near the boys). Frank laid his things out neatly on the bed and shaved the stubble off his face in the bathroom with the razor we gave him. He was sweet, a bit sheepish, and not too proud to be grateful.

The next morning, Frank came upstairs smiling and ate breakfast with our family. He chatted with the boys and gave them a deck of cards from his backpack. We gave him a Bible.

Frank said he couldn't remember when he'd had a more peaceful night's sleep. (And our hide-a-bed is pretty lumpy, I'm just saying.) Then Shane took him to the station. Frank called us three days later to say he'd made it to Portland. He has called a couple more times over the years.

The Spirit seems to be transforming his life, just like He's transforming mine. (Obviously, I needed some work.) The Holy Spirit excels in transformations of all kinds, so I shouldn't be surprised. As Jesus promised his disciples, "Very truly I tell you, whoever believes in me will do the works I have been doing, and they will do even greater things than these, because I am going to the Father."[66] Jesus leaves us with a powerful tool. Even his disciples did not understand or know how to utilize the Holy Spirit, so Jesus explained,

> "All this I have spoken while still with you. But the Counselor, the Holy Spirit, whom the Father will send in my name, will teach you all things and will remind you of everything I have said to you. Peace I leave with you; my peace I give you. I do not give to you as the world gives. Do not let your hearts be troubled and do not be afraid . . . . I will not speak with you much longer, for the prince of this world is coming. He has no hold on me, but the world must learn that I love the Father and that I do exactly what my Father has commanded."[67]

What great advice for living powerful lives: Don't be afraid. Access the Spirit. Anticipate the Devil. Win the battle. Obey God. Pray the longings of your soul and spirit.

Then Jesus showed them how to do it. And he changed their destinies.

Two thousand years later, His plan hasn't changed. In His love and mercy, God allows us to join Him in this incredible work some call "spiritual warfare," and He empowers us to do the unimaginable. Francis Schaeffer explained the tension like this: "We . . . are locked in a battle. This is not a friendly, gentleman's discussion. It is a life and death conflict between the spiritual hosts of wickedness and those who claim the name of Christ."[68] If we refuse to acknowledge the spiritual battle that commences around us, we will become casualties of that war. Pretending the war doesn't exist won't protect us at all.

> "God is not fighting the Devil to beat him. Jesus has already beaten him. God wars against the Devil to win us!"

Spiritual warfare is simply the battle between Satan and God, which began with the Devil's determination to become God and God's response of ejecting him from heaven.[69] They have been waging war for the souls of mankind ever since. The Devil, in strategy to prevent men from recognizing and accepting Jesus' love, has created a world system that guilts us, depresses us, lies to us, and enslaves us to our sin nature, making it difficult—even highly improbable—to accept the possibility of forgiveness and freedom in Christ.

But the Devil underestimates God's passion. "For God so loved the world that He gave His one and only Son, that whoever believes in Him should not perish, but have eternal life."[70] God is not fighting the Devil to beat him. Jesus has already beaten him. God wars against the Devil *to win us*! He has been on a quest to win back humanity since the Devil slithered out of the Garden of Eden.

The Devil doesn't realize it, but the redemption story was written before he lied to Eve. God had provided the ultimate Protagonist and His climactic confrontation against the antagonist. The theme of God's great story was love and redemption. He intended all along to sacrifice Himself in love for His creation, to rescue mankind from the enemy's grasp. "For this purpose the Son of God was manifested, that he might destroy the works of the devil."[71]

Destroy is a powerful word in the Greek: "taken from the Greek word *luo*, and it refers to 'the act of untying or loosing something.' It is the exact word we would use to picture a person who is untying his shoes. In fact, the word *luo* is used in this exact way in Luke 3:16, when John the Baptist says, 'but one mightier than I cometh, the latchet of whose shoes I am not worthy to *unloose* . . . .' Thus, Jesus Christ came into the world to *untie* and *unloose* Satan's binding powers over us. At the cross, Jesus unraveled Satan's power until His redemptive work was finally complete and our liberty was fully purchased."[72]

By loosening the Devil's grip, God destroys his chance to control you. Satan's not in charge of you, no matter how powerful he looks. Jesus promised that "whoever believes in me will do the works I have been doing, and they will do even greater things than these, because I am going to the Father."[73] God plans to do *greater things* through us than He did through Jesus!

How is that even possible?

THE ART OF WAR

When my boys were kids, they loved war. Not real war—which they have thankfully never experienced, just the concept of war—the glorified struggle between good and evil, heroes and villains, glory and defeat.

They played board games like Stratego, Risk, and Battleship. They played Star Wars, cops and robbers, army, and superheroes. Some of my fondest memories of the boys involved them streaking through the house wearing their Superman or Batman pajamas, glancing backward to catch a glimpse of their capes floating behind them. For a good decade, we had an entire closet devoted to weapons and costumes. All their friends made a beeline for that closet whenever they came to play. They all wanted to fight epic battles, and they all planned to win.

However, when I was a brand-new mother, I had initially banned war paraphernalia. I determined that we would not allow toy guns in the house. I did not want to advocate violence.

Then I caught my toddler son reaching into a kitchen drawer to take out a straw. He bent it and pointed the long end toward the wall and made a shooting noise. (To my knowledge, he had never seen a gun in a movie or a TV show.) He turned sticks into pistols. He waved branches for swords while wearing his football helmet.

Don't judge me, but I bought the boys plastic suits of knight's armor and began reading them more books about castles. Of course, I taught them about the armor of God from Ephesians 6, so that purified the warfare, in my mind. The boys began learning Scripture verses around age three, and we used a sticker verse chart to keep track of the verses they could quote to me. On Saturdays, we tallied up the verse stickers and went to Target and picked out a treat.

Why talk about warfare? Because kids need to understand that for the rest of their lives, they are in a spiritual war (you don't need to buy armor or play with guns to teach this, by the way). Our kids must fight against deceit by guarding their hearts and minds with God's truth. C. S. Lewis wrote, "There is no neutral ground in the universe; every square inch, every split second is claimed by God and counterclaimed by Satan."[74] The Devil will twist every one of God's truths, so we must all make sure we can tell truth from lies.

Paul explains the conflict in military terms.

"Finally, be strong in the Lord and in his mighty power. Put on the full armor of God so that you can take your stand against the devil's evil schemes. For our struggle is not against flesh and blood, but against the rulers, against the authorities, against the powers of this dark world and against the spiritual forces of evil in the heavenly realms."[75]

The spiritual forces of evil are gunning for you, whether you think about them or not. The Devil and his demons have thousands of years of experience studying the psyche of mankind; they know what to do. Your enemy knows your lustful fantasies; he understands your pride and insecurity. He knows exactly what tempts you, what deceives you, and what allures you into thinking that dangerous things are harmless, and over-vigilance is prudish extremism. The Devil is an expert in the craft of spiritual warfare. You should be, too.

I am so thankful that I am already a victor because Christ lives in me, and His power trumps anything the Devil or his demons can throw my way! "Draw nigh to God; resist the devil, and he will flee from you."[76] Beating the Devil occurs through your intimacy with the Father, but resisting takes some strategic preparation.

HOW TO PREPARE FOR SPIRITUAL WARFARE

Paul, as a missionary, encountered spiritual opposition everywhere he preached the gospel. Just read the book of Acts. He didn't run away, nor did he pretend that apathy greeted him in every pagan city. His opposition came straight from the pit of hell, and Paul met it head-on. "For our struggle is not against flesh and blood, but against the rulers, against the authorities, against the powers of this dark world and against the spiritual forces of evil in the heavenly realms."[77] The Devil will go down, but he'll go down swinging. And he'll take as many with him as he can. This is why we must battle.

Paul breaks down the components of fighting your spiritual enemy with the metaphor of a soldier going to war. You must strap on your armor for a spiritual fight. You must arm yourself to avoid the death and destruction that your enemy has planned for you.

When Paul describes each piece of armor, he highlights the imagery of its characteristics. Your spiritual warfare involves resisting, not attacking, the Devil. (Are you breathing easier?) Even Jesus, during two powerful spiritual assaults from the Devil,[78] met His enemy in a defensive posture. Your success doesn't depend on your experience or your cunning—only on your preparation to fulfill your mission.

> "Therefore, put on the full armor of God, so that when the day of evil comes, you may be able to stand your ground, and after you have done everything, to stand. Stand firm then, with the belt of truth buckled around your waist, with the breastplate of righteousness in place, and with your feet fitted with the readiness that comes from the gospel of peace. In addition to all this, take up the shield of faith, with which you can extinguish all the flaming arrows of the evil one. Take the helmet of salvation and the sword of the Spirit, which is the word of God. And pray in the Spirit on all occasions with all kinds of prayers and requests. With this in mind, be alert and always keep on praying for all the Lord's people. Pray also for me, that whenever I speak, words may be given me so that I will fearlessly make known the mystery of the gospel, for which I am an ambassador in chains. Pray that I may declare it fearlessly, as I should."[79]

While most of the armor appears protective in nature, each piece is worn because the soldier who wears it *is progressing toward battle.* He is not hiding behind city walls reading his manual and restricting his interaction to comrades like himself. He is dressed and ready to march—into conflict, against a powerful enemy! Why would defensive soldiers march *toward* battle? Perhaps our engagement is more about showing up and letting God do His work than it is about being powerful Christians.

You were wondering how all this warfare tied into prayer, weren't you? Warfare begins with prayer, continues under prayer, and ends with prayer. Of all the weapons we carry, prayer remains the most valuable because it connects us to our Commander. It's how we recognize our enemy and defeat him.

P.R.A.Y.

To help you remember how to wage spiritual warfare with your prayers, use the acrostic **PRAY**. These four steps will help you face the forces of evil and vanquish them through the power of the Holy Spirit. Jesus' prayer in the Garden of Gethsemane provides a powerful example.[80]

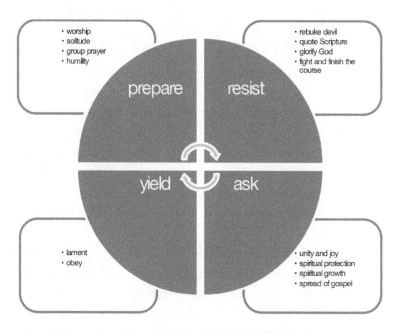

Prepare. Jesus led the disciples in a hymn (worship), went to a quiet place (solitude), employed prayer partners (prayer group), knelt down (humility), and prayed for courage (request). He recognized His enemy and fortified Himself for the attack that was coming.

Resist. In many instances throughout His life, Jesus had rebuked the Devil, commanded demons to flee, and quoted Scripture. However, during the moments before His greatest trial, He prayed to glorify God. He saw the impending attack, and He braced Himself through reminders to stay the course—to glorify God at all costs, to fulfill God's will. When Paul neared the end of his life in a dank prison cell, he spoke similar words: "For I am already being poured out like a drink offering, and the time has come for my departure. I have fought a good fight, I have finished the race, I have kept the faith."[81]

Nothing will help you resist the Devil more than a life poured out to God. You must flee temptation, but you must not flee spiritual warfare. That is not how you win. When the Devil confronts your calling and challenges your destiny in Christ, dig in, get your shield up, and raise your sword. You can beat him. It's God's will for you to beat him.

Ask. Jesus made several requests in his final agonizing prayer. He prayed for the disciples to have unity and joy (not large congregations and fancy programs); He prayed for His followers' safety (from the world's influence, not from the world's persecution); He prayed for His followers' spiritual growth and influence (not fame, fortune, or ease); and He prayed for future believers to know and be known by Him (that's us!).

Yield. When Jesus prayed for His "cup to pass," He wasn't asking God to airlift him from His mission. He was lamenting over His coming separation from His Father—that horrifying and humiliating moment when He would experience the sins of the universe and subsequent alienation from God. In Luke 14:36, Jesus prayed earnestly, while blood oozed from His pores, "Abba, Father, everything is possible for You. Take this cup from Me, yet not My will, but Yours be done." He implores with the most familiar title, *Abba*, the Greek equivalent of *Daddy,* which shows not only love, but also dependence. Jesus is lamenting, "Daddy, please help me! I'm afraid to do this, but I will, because this was your plan, and I will obey you."

This same Jesus intercedes for us in heaven right now. He turns to Jehovah God and says, "Dad, I died for her. I cover her sins. Forgive her sins and answer her requests." He's the same Jesus who confronts demons and sends them packing. The Protector and the Powerful. The Intercessor and the Conqueror. He's the one I submit myself to, not from fear or obligation, but from awe and reverence.

I don't have the right to question His purposes. He has already proven Himself faithful at the cross. He has nothing more to prove to me.

ON THE FRONT LINES

Spiritual warfare requires a mature and practiced prayer life. Remember, the Devil bows under the authority of Jesus' name, not your attempts to represent Him. Matthew 17:14-21 and Mark 9:14-29 relate the story of well-intentioned disciples entering a spiritual battle unarmed.

> "When they came to the other disciples, they saw a large crowd around them and the teachers of the law arguing with them. As soon as all the people saw Jesus, they were overwhelmed with wonder and ran to greet him.
>
> 'What are you arguing with them about?' he asked.
>
> A man in the crowd answered, 'Teacher, I brought you my son, who is possessed by a spirit that has robbed him of speech. Whenever it seizes him, it throws him to the ground. He foams at the mouth, gnashes his teeth and becomes rigid. I asked your disciples to drive out the spirit, but they could not.'
>
> 'You unbelieving generation,' Jesus replied, 'how long shall I stay with you? How long shall I put up with

you? Bring the boy to me.'

So they brought him. When the spirit saw Jesus, it immediately threw the boy into a convulsion. He fell to the ground and rolled around, foaming at the mouth. Jesus asked the boy's father, 'How long has he been like this?'

'From childhood,' he answered. 'It has often thrown him into fire or water to kill him. But if you can do anything, take pity on us and help us.'

' "If you can"?' said Jesus. 'Everything is possible for one who believes.'

Immediately the boy's father exclaimed, 'I do believe; help me overcome my unbelief!'

When Jesus saw that a crowd was running to the scene, he rebuked the impure spirit. 'You deaf and mute spirit,' he said, 'I command you, come out of him and never enter him again.'

The spirit shrieked, convulsed him violently and came out. The boy looked so much like a corpse that many said, 'He's dead.'

But Jesus took him by the hand and lifted him to his feet, and he stood up.

After Jesus had gone indoors, his disciples asked him privately, 'Why couldn't we drive it out?'

He replied, 'This kind can come out only by prayer.'

In the parallel Scripture, Jesus elaborates on the response like this: "Because you have so little faith. Truly I tell you, if you have faith as small as a mustard seed, you can say to this mountain, 'Move from here to there,' and it will move. Nothing will be impossible for you."

Nothing will be impossible!

I'M NOT STRONG ENOUGH

Okay, that's enough. You're freaking me out. I'm not strong enough to summon Holy Spirit power and vanquish evil. That's crazy stuff.

Good. Then you realize that spiritual warfare is an act of the Spirit of God. You are merely a conduit. God doesn't need to use you, but He loves to use you. He won't hurry you, but He might whisper in your ear, "You can do it. Just pray over that person. I'll hear you."

So you pray. And it works. (You are now a warrior!)

READY FOR COMBAT?

Daniel was ready. From the moment he was taken captive to Babylon (Daniel Chapter 1), Daniel, as well as Shadrach, Meshach, and Abednego, had remained faithful to Jewish laws. As much as "fitting in" would secure a place in a new kingdom, Daniel and his friends had each determined to remain holy and set apart for God's mission.

Several Old Testament books are filled with amazing stories of the heroes from the Babylonian/Persian kingdoms; in addition to Daniel, Hananiah, Mishael, and Azariah, other leaders like Mordecai, Ezra, Esther, and Nehemiah also joined the ranks of Jews who worshipped Jehovah at great risk. In the midst of an oppressive environment, these spiritual warriors maintained a relationship with God that drove them to their knees in *soulspeak*. They didn't have to rebel against their captors because God waged war on their behalf and made them succeed in their missions.

In Daniel's life, you can trace a power and blessing back to a practice of prayer and fasting. Daniel describes one of many incredible revelations from God:

> "While I was speaking and praying, confessing my sin and the sin of my people Israel and making my request to the Lord my God for his holy hill—while I was still in prayer, Gabriel, the man I had seen in the earlier vision, came to me in swift flight about the time of the evening sacrifice. He instructed me and said to me, 'Daniel, I

have now come to give you insight and understanding. As soon as you began to pray, a word went out, which I have come to tell you, for you are highly esteemed.'"

As soon as he began to pray, God sent *Gabriel* to answer him! Holy smokes! Daniel praised, confessed, requested, and interceded for his people, and God sent the archangel to answer him.

Nehemiah was ready. Given the dangerous and important job of the king's cupbearer (food-tester), Nehemiah records the king's response to his sadness over Jerusalem's ruin in this story:

> "The king said to me, 'What is it you want?'
> Then I prayed to the God of heaven, and I answered the king, 'If it pleases the king and if your servant has found favor in his sight, let him send me to the city in Judah where my fathers are buried so that I can rebuild it.'"

Nehemiah would engage in spiritual warfare against Sanballat, Tobiah, and the other enemies surrounding Jerusalem, yet would complete his miraculous mission. He would rebuild God's city in only 52 days, and Persia would pay for it. What mission is pressing on your heart that God wants to build and fund?

REVIEW OF SPIRITUAL WARFARE

- You are in a spiritual battle, either fighting for God or with the Devil

- You must defend your heart and mind from the Devil

- You can fight for other people and events

- God has already won the victory you're fighting for—He just wants your participation

- Prayer is the best defense against spiritual enemies

PRAYERS OF SPIRITUAL WARFARE

Consider Paul's prayer of warfare below and pray a similar prayer of spiritual warfare.

Paul's prayer in Acts 16:18-30:
Finally Paul became so troubled that he turned around and said to the spirit, "In the name of Jesus Christ, I command you to come out of her!" At that moment the spirit left her. When the owners of the slave girl realized that their hope of making money was gone, they seized Paul and Silas . . . and the magistrates ordered them to be stripped and beaten. After they had been severely flogged, they were thrown into prison . . . About midnight Paul and Silas were praying and singing hymns to God, and the other prisoners were listening to them. Suddenly there was a violent earthquake . . . The jailer called for lights, rushed in and fell trembling before Paul and Silas. . . "Sirs, what must I do to be saved?"

My prayer from Acts 16:
God of heaven and earth, Who retains all power to change hearts and save lives—make me more like Yourself! Fill me with the power of the Holy Spirit so that I can serve You and help others! In Jesus' name, I command _____ to _____. I bind the enemy of God in Jesus' name. He will not gain control over _____. I pray in Jesus' name for _____ to be saved/returned to your control, to be renewed in the image of Your Son, Jesus, who deserves all our praise, all glory on earth, and all majesty in heaven. In the powerful name of Jesus, Amen.

PART 9:
THE UNEXPECTED
PLACES

WE'VE BEEN TALKING about change for a while now. You picked up this book hoping to pray change into your life. Perhaps you've discovered something different, something delightfully unexpected.

This new heart, this heart that leans into raw emotions, builds patterns that layer personal entreaties and confessions on a foundation of praise. Your prayers have guided you toward the Creator and Sustainer of life, the Beginning and the End, the Bridegroom, the Everlasting Father, the Comforter, the Friend, the Teacher, the Master, the Prince of Peace, the Great I AM. God has opened His arms and enfolded you. He is everything you need, exactly when you need Him.

I hope you've discovered your *soulspeak*—your own patterns for prayer, uttered from your strongest fears and deepest longings, lifted to God's throne with clean hands and pure hearts.

Will you allow your soul's hoarse whispers to scratch tiny alterations to your thoughts and beliefs? Will you let the Holy Spirit speak change into the dark corners and musty dungeons of your soul, bringing rays of light and hope and destiny?

Change happens daily, as you pray.

You can still pray spontaneously. I do. I pray protection over my children and patience with my work. But I must also choose to lament for the woman who's going through a divorce or the teenager who's partying hard on the weekends. I must choose to admit and confess my own sins instead of judge theirs. If humility does not become my way of life, my prayers will be powerless.

I must choose to be like Jesus every day. *Every moment.* Because every minute my human nature wants to focus on myself—what I want, why I deserve it, and why God should give it to me. *Every moment.* It's exhausting how much I love myself.

I am really that self-centered. You probably are, too.

Maybe you could consider incorporating at least one thing from each of these chapters, gradually, without pressuring yourself with aspirations of perfection. Focus on one prayer type per week or per month until it becomes a habit. Pick one takeaway and write it on a 3x5 card and tape it where you'll read it every day, like on your mirror or your dashboard. Each day, read it, pray over it, choose it. Don't worry about the life change that will transform you into a mighty prayer warrior. God will do that work. All you need to do is obey and make choices that move you gradually toward a radically altered life.

Unless you are inspired by hyper-organization, avoid the ambitions to make lists and calendars to schedule your new ideals. Don't expect to muster the willpower you've never had before. Instead, pick a few simple truths and commit them to God.

Here are seven practical, measurable, takeaway truths, one for each prayer type, to help you implement change into your spiritual routine:

- Praise: Listen to a song that praises God; then thank Him for His character. Listen to different songs that celebrate varying aspects of His character.
- Confession: Whenever you sin, call your action by its real name, no excuses allowed. Ask forgiveness for *that.*

- Lament: Pinpoint an area of grief and get counseling for it.
- Thanksgiving: Be humble and give something away every day (time, money, things). Your kids don't count as receivers. Give to other people, people you don't know or don't even like.
- Request: Find a prayer partner and be transparent about your needs. Meet regularly and pray together.
- Intercession: Schedule a period of solitude every week or every month. Spend an hour or two in a park or in your yard; read a psalm and listen to God.
- Spiritual Warfare: Start memorizing Bible verses. Write each one on a card so you can review them.

As you change, you will notice things around you changing. You will begin to see the miraculous power of God everywhere you look. You will see Him in your home and at your workplace, in your church and in your neighborhood. You will see Him transforming fallen beings into reflections of Himself—converting lives, one crisis at a time. You will begin to believe that you can make a difference by praying. You will read the book of Acts and not be shocked that 13 apostles turned the world upside down, amidst persecution and poverty. That over the centuries, women and men have received inspiration, faced inquisitions, preached deliverance, endured torture, smuggled Bibles, and fought injustice.

Regular men and women like you have changed history because they prayed.

I wonder what your prayers will do?

DISCUSSION QUESTIONS

Use these discussion questions for Bible studies, book clubs, or personal use.

Part 1: What is *Soulspeak?*

1. Share or contemplate your spiritual background. What did you grow up expecting God to do for you?
2. Review your experience with prayer, beginning as a child. How important was prayer to your daily routine or your spiritual experience?
3. Can you remember times when your soul longed to communicate with God? Describe what happened and how it impacted your view of God and prayer.

Part 2: "You're Awesome!": Speaking Praise

1. Discuss your view of God's goodness. How do you think God is connected to the good and bad things that happen to you and around you?
2. In what ways are you comfortable worshipping God? Discuss different forms of worship. Which forms of praise are you willing to incorporate into your personal worship experience?
3. Discuss your fear or anxiety about praising God for who He is instead of what He does. Discuss strategies for how you can replace fear with courage.
4. Describe a time in your life when your adoration of God's character gave you the courage to move forward

through a trial. How did this experience impact you? Share the experience with others.

Part 3: "My Bad": Speaking Confession

1. Analyze your pattern of confession and repentance. Discuss how you take responsibility for your sins or how you excuse / rename them.
2. Pick a sin habit that troubles you. What, if any, systems do you have in place for prevention and accountability? How can you implement the Put off/Put on principle from Eph. 4?
3. Discuss the concept of asking, giving, and receiving forgiveness. How does this process liberate relationships? How can you improve in this area?
4. Discuss the difficulties of forgiveness when one party is not remorseful or repentant. How can prayer help heal you, regardless of the other person's response?
5. Consider the prayer of confession for salvation from sins. Share about when you asked God for His forgiveness of your sins or discuss why you're having difficulty praying this prayer.
6. Analyze the connection between confession of sins and feelings of entitlement. How does confession interfere with your perspective on God's blessing?

Part 4: "Life Stinks": Speaking Lamentation

1. Discuss the difference between *crying to God* and *crying out to God*. Which form of complaint are you most likely to employ? Why?
2. How does lamenting help you to consider God's perspective and will? How would accepting God's authority in your life help you to handle crises and make wise decisions?
3. Discuss the proofs in Scripture that God wants to heal our wounds. Do you have trouble believing that? Why?

4. Discuss grief and how it affects you. Can you think of a grief that you have been unable to deal with in a healthy manner? Consider sharing this burden with your group and formulating a plan for recovery.

Part 5: "Thanks a Bunch": Speaking Thanksgiving

1. How does humility play a crucial part in becoming thankful for everything?
2. Consider the personal difficulties involved with living a life of humility. What areas of your life are hard to surrender to God's control? What measures could you take to surrender them?
3. Discuss the enslaving aspect of discontentment. When have you felt enslaved by your wants? Consider what hinders you from surrendering them.
4. Discuss the lifestyle or attitude changes necessary to live a life of thankfulness and contentment.
5. Discuss the impact of generosity on greed and thank-lessness. Share stories of generosity, from your own life or from someone else's.

Part 6: "Pretty Please": Speaking Requests

1. Review what prayer attitudes and actions need to be practiced before a request should be made.
2. How has praying with praise, confession, lament, and thanksgiving transformed your prayer requests?
3. Discuss the process of discerning God's will. How does God reveal His will for us? How does He show us where we should invest our time and energy?
4. Discuss the benefits and risks involved in sharing prayer requests in a group format. What steps can you take to overcome the fear of sharing your requests with others?
5. How do thanksgiving and requesting fit together? How can they affect one another in producing power-ful prayers?

Part 7: "Someone Needs Your Help": Speaking Intercession

1. According to the chart, what is the 3-fold path to effective intercession? Which step is the hardest for you?
2. Discuss the importance of solitude in hearing and discerning God's voice.
3. Discuss the interdependence of discernment, fasting, prayer, and solitude. Which area is new or uncomfortable for you? How can you move forward in this area?
4. Analyze what you perceive to be the motive behind intercession and the blessing of intercession. Why do you think intercession bears significance to the heart of God?

Part 8: "Back off, Buster!": Speaking Spiritual Warfare

1. Prior to this chapter, what were your impressions of spiritual warfare and the devil? Have any of your impressions changed? Please explain.
2. Discuss the role of prayer in spiritual warfare.
3. Explain and discuss the process of defending yourself against the enemy's attacks with the spiritual armor in Eph. 6. Which piece of armor is currently most important to your fight and why? How can the Put off/ Put on principle in Eph. 4 help you fight and win?
4. Discuss why we should fight spiritual battles with boldness and courage. Consider how your trust in God's character affects your courage to fight the enemy. How does your faith build or weaken your courage?

Part 9: Prayer that Changes Everything

1. Discuss how studying the prayer has affected your life. What has been the biggest area of change in your spiritual life?
2. What spiritual goals are you setting for yourself? Share your strategy for living a spirit-controlled life and/or praying more productively.

SOURCES

Alves, Elizabeth. *Becoming a Prayer Warrior.* Ventura, CA: Regal, 1998. 48, 69.

Bible Hub, "Abba." http://biblehub.com/greek/5.htm

Blueletterbible.org.   https://www.blueletterbible.org/lang/lexicon/lexicon.cfm?Strongs=G1381&t=NIV
https://www.blueletterbible.org/lang/lexicon/lexicon.cfm?Strongs=H7993&t=NIV

Cymbala, Jim. *When God's People Pray.* Grand Rapids, MI: Zondervan, 2007. 86

Guranlink, David B. , Ed. in Chief. *Webster's New World Dictionary*, 2nd Ed. New York: Prentice Hall, 1984. 790.

Keller, Tim. *Prayer: Experiencing Awe and Intimacy with God.* New York: Penguin, 2014, 5.

Lewis, C. S. Walter Hooper, Ed. "Christianity and Culture." *Christian Reflections.* Grand Rapids, MI: Eerdmans, 1995. 33.

Lewis, C. S. Walter Hooper, Ed. *The Collected Letters of C.S. Lewis, Volume 2: Books, Broadcasts, and War, 1931-1949.* San Francisco: Harper Collins, 2004. Aug. 10, 1948, 869.

Peterson, Eugene H., trans. *The Message: The Bible in Contemporary Language.* Colorado Springs, CO: NavPress, 2016.

Pink, A.W. *The Sovereignty of God.* Blacksburg, VA: Wilder Publications, 2009, 124.

Renner, Rick. "Taking the Mystery Out of Spiritual Warfare." Adapted from *Dressed to Kill* by Rick Renner. *Believer's Voice of Victory* Magazine, May 15, 2014, 22-25.

Harry S. Truman Library and Museum. http://www.trumanlibrary.org/buckstop.htm

Schaeffer, Francis. *A Christian View of the Church, Vol. 4* in *The Complete Words of Francis Schaeffer: A Christian Worldview.* Wheaton, IL: Crossway, 1982, 316.

Spurgeon, Charles H. "The Wailing of Risca." No. 349. A Sermon Delivered on December 9, 1860.

Voskamp, Ann. *One Thousand Gifts. Grand Rapids, MI:* Zondervan, 2010. 72, 175.

Webster, Daniel. *Webster's The New World Dictionary of the American Language.* 2nd Ed. New York: Prentice Hall, 1986. 733, 790.

ENDNOTES

1 https://www.blueletterbible.org/niv/gen/24/24/t_conc_24019

2 Tim Keller, *Prayer: Experiencing Awe and Intimacy with God*, New York: Penguin, 2014, 5.

3 Hebrews 11:6

4 Harry S Truman Library, http://www.trumanlibrary.org/buckstop.htm

5 Mothers of Preschoolers is an international program for reaching mothers of preschool children through fellowship, encouragement, spiritual growth, and rest from mothering.

6 Isaiah 53:3

7 John 16:33

8 Ann Voskamp, *One Thousand Gifts,* Grand Rapids, MI: Zondervan, 2010, 175

9 David Guranlink, Ed. in Chief, *Webster's New World Dictionary*, 2nd Ed., New York: Prentice Hall, 1984, 790

10 Job 1:1, NLT

11 Job 42:1-6

12 John 15:13

13 Psalm 34:17-18

14 Isaiah 61:1 and Luke 4:17-19

15 Psalms 3, 5, 6, 7,10, 13, 14, 17, 22, 34, 54, 56, 57, 59, 63, 70, 71, 109, 141, and 142 are all laments of David. Many other psalms contain verses of lamentation.

16 Lamentations 3:7-8, 21-24

17 John 13:35

18 John 3:16

19 Luke 5:13

20 Luke 17:11

21 Luke 17:17

22 Deuteronomy 8:1

23 Philippians 3:7-11, Peterson, Eugene H., trans. *The Message: The Bible in Contemporary Language,* Colorado Springs, CO: NavPress, 2016.

24 Philippians 3:18, 20

25 C. S. Lewis, in a letter to Don Giovanni Calabria V, Aug. 10, 1948; *The Collected Letters of C.S. Lewis, Volume 2: Books, Broadcasts, and War, 1931-3949 by C. S. Lewis,* San Francisco: Harper Collins, 2004, 869.

26 1 Timothy 6:6

27 Philippians 4:6-7

28 Psalm 107:8, 15, 21

29 Daniel 6:10-11

30 Philippians 2:5-11

31 A.W. Pink, *The Sovereignty of God,* Blacksburg, VA: Wilder Publications, 2009, 124.

32 Matthew 7:7-11

33 Galatians 6:1, Peterson, Eugene H., trans. *The Message: The Bible in Contemporary Language.*

34 1 Thessalonians 5:18

35 Psalm 24:3-5

36 Isa. 55:9 (NLT)

37 Mark 9:18-20

38 *Webster's New World Dictionary,* 733

39 1 John 4:1, www.blueletterbible.org

40 John 13:35

41 Ephesians 6:18

42 Charles Spurgeon, Sermon 349, "The Wailing of Risca"

43 John 13:34

44 Matthew 18:20

45 These stories are found in the book of Daniel.

46 These stories are found in the book of Esther.

47 The first church is described in Acts 1-12. Acts 9:2 references the early church's name, called "the Way."

48 Exodus 33:11

49 Galatians 5:22-23

50 ibid, 5:25

51 This story is recorded in 1 Samuel 3. Samuel is command-ed by God himself to deliver a message to Eli. The message confirmed God's wrath and punishment of Eli's wicked sons and on Eli for not correcting them when they sinned.

52 Job 42:1-5

53 Job 42:7-8

54 James 2:23

55 1 Peter 2:8

56 Genesis 18 tells the story of Abraham bargaining with God for the salvation of Sodom and Gomorrah, strictly because he wanted God to spare his nephew's family.

57 Luke 4:42-44, Mark 1:35-45, Matthew 14:13-36, and Mark 6:31-56 tell stories of healings, miracles, and exorcisms fol-lowing Jesus' prayer time in solitude.

58 2 Corinthians 11:14

59 Elizabeth Alves, *Becoming a Prayer Warrior*, Ventura, CA: Regal, 1998, 69.

60 Luke 11:9-11

61 Luke 11:23-26

62 Luke 14:12

63 John 14:25-27, 30-31

64 Francis Schaeffer, *A Christian View of the Church*, Vol. 4, *The Complete Words of Francis Schaeffer: A Chrsitian Worldview*, Wheaton: IL: Crossway, 1982, 316.

65 Ezekiel 28

66 John 3:16

67 1 John 3:8

68 Rick Renner, "Taking the Mystery Out of Spiritual War-fare." *BVOV Magazine*, May 15, 2014, 22-25.

69 John 14:12

70 C. S. Lewis, "Christianity and Culture," *Christian Reflec-tions*, Grand Rapids, MI, 1995, 33.

71 Ephesians 6:12

72 James 4:7

73 Ephesians 6:12

74 Satan tempted Jesus in the wilderness three times (Matthew 4) and waged war against him as He submitted to the crucifixion, in the Garden of Gethsemene and on Golgotha (John 17-19).

75 Ephesians 6:13-20

76 John 17

77 2 Timothy 4:6

78 "*Abbá* – Father, also used as the term of *tender endearment* by a beloved child – i.e. in an *affectionate, dependent* relationship with their father; '*daddy*,' '*papa*.'"—www.biblehub.com.

79 Matthew 17:20

80 Daniel 9:20-23

81 Nehemiah 2:4

CPSIA information can be obtained
at www.ICGtesting.com
Printed in the USA
LVHW092302130919
631090LV00001B/60/P